1980

IRAN'S REVOLUTIONARY UPHEAVAL

An Interpretive Essay

By Sepehr Zabih

IBN 0-931290-18-X
(Hardcover)

ISBN 0-931290-19-8
(Paperback)

Library of Congress No. 79-53696

ALCHEMY BOOKS

681 Market Street
San Francisco, CA 94105

PREFACE

Over the last four years the author has been involved in systematic research on Iran's political development. With the coauthorship of his second major work in 1974, entitled *The Foreign Relations of Iran,* he changed his emphasis from foreign relations to domestic political development. Beginning in 1975 he started work on the problem of political participation and alienation of politically significant strata of the Iranian population.

In the summer of 1978 while finishing touches were being put on a manuscript on "Iran's unique one-party system," the revolutionary upheaval that began in January of that year necessitated the incorporation of that study into the present manuscript. It was in the course of this study that many of the incipient causes of the forthcoming turmoil were identified. Fieldwork in Iran both in January and June-July of that year enabled the author to utilize original sources and conduct numerous lengthy interviews with political leaders, university professors, diplomats and journalists, many of whom were destined to play leading roles in the yearlong revolutionary upheaval.

The introduction outlines the main focus of this inquiry. Chapter one examines the dilemma of political participation in an autocratic country. Chapters two and three discuss the religious dimension of the upheaval and the interrelated issue of politicization of the bazaar's tradesmen and merchants. Chapter four examines the economic mismanagement and its resulting severe disparity, while chapter five reviews the opposition groups and their modes of challenging the Iranian political system. Chapter six is devoted to the four stages of the revolutionary process, stressing the strategy and tactics utilized by the revolutionary forces and the relative contributions of each to the regime's ultimate destruction. The disintegration of the military in the last stage is covered as one of the significant immediate causes for the revolution's triumph. The concluding chapter characterizes the Iranian revolution and a postscript follows the events of the first few months of revolutionary government.

This study was facilitated by the renewal of the author's research associateship at the Institute of International Studies, University of California, Berkeley, and a sabattical leave from St. Mary's College, Moraga. The first continued his access to research facilities here and abroad, while the second freed him from teaching responsibilities at a time that fast developing events in Iran required constant and undivided concentration. Neither, of course, is responsible for the contents of this study.

The author wishes to express his gratitude to Mr. Joel Walters, formerly of the University of California Press, for competent editing of this manuscript.

CONTENTS

Introduction

The year long revolutionary turmoil which finally toppled the Iranian ruling regime in February 1979 is not unique in modern Iranian history. In fact it is the third such disruption in the twentieth century. After the first of these, which began in 1906, the absolutist dynasty of Qajar (1794-1925) was compelled to accede to the demands of "Constitutionalists" who wished to establish a limited government modeled on European parliamentary monarchies such as that of Belgium. That Constitutional Revolution, which lasted until 1911, was supervened by events of World War I, and in its wake in 1925 the Pahlavi dynasty was founded.

The second disorder occurred in the early 1950's when a nationalist movement mobilized the people around the nationalization of the oil industry and used this mobilization to curb the practically unlimited powers of the second ruler of the Pahlavi dynasty. This movement, led by Dr. Mohammad Mossadegh and his National Front, was no more successful than the Constitutional Revolution of nearly half a century earlier. A combination of economic hardship resulting from an oil embargo by the Western oil cartel and foreign intervention formented by the CIA in opposition to an alleged communist threat to Iran put an end to the nationalist movement and reinstated the Shah.

For nearly a quarter of a century he ruled with progressively repressive absolutism. In the intervening period several abortive attempts were made to challenge the Shah's authority, but none succeeded and some even proved counterproductive in that they provided justification for further repressive measures.

In order to understand the nature and cause of Iran's third revolutionary upheaval in this century, several critical questions should be raised. Among them are: How and why did the authority of the regime gradually erode and ultimately disintegrate? How did a protest movement become a revolutionary upheaval? Why did the Iranian system fail to defuse the revolutionary turmoil by timely and perceptive accommodation with the forces of opposition?

Certain questions commonly posed during the last few months of 1978 were particularly illustrative of the general bewilderment. What went wrong? How was Iran lost? These questions reflected certain basic assumptions, not the least of which was that for the most part the Iranian crisis was unexpected.

Neither the intelligence community nor the academic world or media sources successfully projected or anticipated the suddenness and depth of the crisis. Conventional wisdom dictated that the Iranian leadership had both sufficient experience and financial resources to cope with the tensions that stemmed from rapid modernization and its resulting stresses and strains. No viable alternative to the Shah was conceivable. With some modest gestures toward the concept of human rights, the regime would continue to assure the survival of this "island of stability in the otherwise turbulent Middle East."

The regime itself was equally euphoric about socio-political conditions. Subversion from conventional sources or a new alliance of black reaction with red Marxism at worst could be treated as a manageable menace and at best as a passing nuisance. It appeared inconceivable that economic growth would generate uncontrollable political consequences. Had not a combination of coercion and cooptation successfully neutralized sources of opposition? Did not the emerging new middle class owe a profound debt of gratitude to its benefactors? If attention were drawn to the lag between political and economic modernization, the creation of the one-party system was offered as the regime's solution to the problem of participation.

In sum, the ship of state was believed to be steering the proper course, navigated by an experienced captain capable of guiding it through the stormy waters of social change to the threshold of a "Great Civilization."[1]

This account will pursue four lines of inquiry and present a summary of how they were interrelated. One will examine the causes and effects of alienation of the politically significant strata of the Iranian population. This analysis begins by an examination of the regime's inability to create a mechanism for political participation without permitting a challenge to its authority.

A second focus of inquiry will be upon the socio-political consequences of economic change which could neither be predicted nor fully controlled.

A third line of inquiry will stress those policies and actions of the regime during its last two years which were designed to stem the tide of the protest movement. The belated liberalization policies, the American sponsorship of human rights, and the Shah's perception of the need to transform his absolutist monarchy into an authoritation-utilitarian system will be analyzed.

The final emphasis will be upon the transformation of the mass protest movement into a revolutionary force and ultimately to an armed insurrection for seizing state power. Participants in this movement, specifically the intelligentsia, the religious hierarchy and the *bazaari* (tradesmen and shopkeepers), the reasons for their gradual radicalization and changes in tactics and strategy will be examined.

In conclusion, the characteristics of the revolution will be assessed together with projections of future prospects.

1

The Dilemma of Political Participation

A fundamental assumption of this study is that the revolutionary upheaval of 1978 was the cumulination of a series of reactions to absolutist monarchical control dating back at least to 1963. This period was characterized by the denial of genuine political participation to the politically significant strata of the Iranian population, even though economic and developmental progress had both expanded these groups and increased their political awareness.

The ruling regime was not altogether unaware of the need for political participation, albeit under controlled conditions. But the difficulty came in devising a system which would make participation safe for the regime. It should be stressed that participation should not be equated with the democratic concepts of accountability or rotation of the ruling elites. The rulers fully understood that this type of participation could easily have resulted in an erosion of their authority. To allow a genuine opposition the freedom to challenge the ruling elite would have permitted questioning the scope and legitimacy of its power. Hence, political participation was confined to competition for political flavors, either by access to the lines of decision-making or by the struggle to occupy strategic positions within the bureaucracy, the military, the business and banking hierarchy, or the government-controlled bicameral parliament.

It was within the latter organization that the regime experimented with the idea of two- and one-party systems, abandoning each when the risk of internal challenge to the regime's authority appeared imminent.

As early as 1958 the Shah introduced the two-party system, with the intention of creating a mechanism of alternation in power of the regime's supporters.[2] Having fully established the authority of the regime and quashed all genuine opposition toward it either from the Marxist left or the nationalist left and center, the government decided that a loyal opposition could be encouraged to develop by participating in parliamentary elections.

By the early 1960's experimentation with a two-party system was abandoned, only to be revived in 1963 with the Shah's initiation of his reform movement. This latter program has been described as the White Revolution or the Shah-People Revolution.

Up to 1975 the ruling party was returned to power in successive elections, often with an increased majority. However, the two-party system, though fully controlled by the regime, did not even achieve its limited objective of rotation of power between the two factions. All it did was create in parliament a loyal opposition which had no prospect of securing the majority in the Majlis and controlling the executive branch of government.

Then in the spring of 1975 upon his return from the OPEC summit conference in Algeria, the Shah abruptly declared that the country now would have a one-party system. The

6

Rastakhiz party, meaning the party of resurgence, was declared the sole legitimate political organization allowed to participate in the upcoming parliamentary elections.

The Shah cited reasons similar to those given by non-Western countries which had transformed a multi-party or two-party system into a one-party system. According to him, the country could not afford the polarization of opinion at a time of intense and wide-ranging modernization. The functioning of the two-party system had undermined national solidarity and threatened a wastage of energy. Unlike Europe, in which class differentiation necessitated multiplication of political parties, Iran had no such class hostility and hence no need for proliferation of political organizations to support their diverse and hostile interests. Furthermore, if a majority of the people selected one political party, why was it necessary to encourage popular disunity? "One country, one Shah and now one party" became the regime's new slogan.

Several additional factors also bear mentioning. The election of the new Majlis was approaching. It was becoming apparent that another victory of Irane Novin party would probably bring about charges of election fraud and ridicule. Why not abandon the pretense of controlled and limited competition between the regime's supporters? The royal authority now believed it no longer needed even a loyal opposition.

Furthermore, a broad mass organization could promote a sense of participation and mobilization that a two-party system could not. Some theorists of the regime even went so far as to suggest that with direct democratic participation, the fear of competitive rivalry and the emergence of a genuine challenge to the regime could be dispelled. In other words, by assuring the regime that no organized effort was being undertaken against it, the people might be trusted to utilize their energies to work within the system. The single party would become a massive interest group, not only participating in the allocation of rewards but functioning as a safety valve for a population increasingly politicized by exposure to the media and shifts to urban centers by the hundreds of thousands.

The regime hoped to be able to confine participation to competition and mobilization for allocation of rewards. It intended that the politically articulate Iranians would acquire a sense of identity with the system, without challenging its monopoly of power or the legitimacy of its policies. Apparently the party was viewed by those in power merely as a mechanism of mass cooptation of alienated or apathetic groups.

The government was encouraged by the success of its selective cooptative efforts toward the intelligentsia.[3] These efforts, accelerated by the 1973 oil boom, generated considerable interests among Western-educated Iranians who were attracted back to the country and who participated actively in business and government. Though never totally depoliticized, they became politically deactivated. Their energies were devoted to making money, either in the public or the private sector of the Iranian economy.

In a sense the regime successfully purchased political apathy, allowing dissident groups to either cooperate with the government or take full advantage of Iran's economic boom. Could the same success be gained vis-a-vis the entire community? Was it necessary to do so? And if so, through what kind of institution? The necessity to coopt more and more of the community stemmed from the need to broaden the basis of government support.

The prospects for success appeared to be very strong, based on experience with the intellectuals. A broad-based political party could extend the same cooptation program to the lower middle class and simultaneously bring it into conformity with the already coopted intelligentsia. By means of the new party, apathetic sectors of the intelligentsia also could be drawn into political participation and indeed assume the leadership role in this state-sponsored political organization.

The Shah was quite blunt in acknowledging the state sponsorship of the new organization and the limitations of political options offered the public. As he saw it, Iranians had the choice of supporting or rejecting the three basic principles of Monarchy, Constitution, and the White Revolution.[4] Supporters now would join the Rastakhiz party to consolidate and promote these objectives. Opponents could either remain apathetic and be non-participants, (in which case they would be denied the fruits of Iran's prosperity); or if they wished to actively oppose these principles, they would be allowed to leave the country.

In short, the new party was now the only means of access to the reward system. All pretense of acceptance of legitimate dissent was abandoned. The one-party system became the essence of "participatory democracy" and the exclusive mechanism of reward distribution.

Though the regime's conception of the functions of the party was clearly understood, the difficulties embodied in such an effort were not so obvious. In the rush of preparations for the new election in June 1975 the party found little time to ponder the practical problems which soon began to plague it. Chief among these were two issues. What would be the relationship between the government structure and the party hierarchy? How could the organization function as a broad interest group without a mechanism for containing its inherent competitive tendencies?

With respect to the first problem, the regime exhibited considerable uncertainty and confusion. It borrowed from the Marxist concept of democratic centralism by trying to structure the new party as an elitist mass party. Participation would be allowed all strata of the public. Leadership, however, would be centered in a tightly organized political bureau which, once elected by the party congress, would be the source of all authority. This authority would flow from the top to the bottom and would not be subject to challenge.

This party differed from other totalitarian single-party systems, since the supreme authority of the Shah was above and beyond it.[5] The Shah was neither accountable to the party nor directly responsible for the possible failure of its policies. On the other hand, the party could function as a buffer to protect the Shah against probable mistakes and mismanagement of the government.

At first, the communist practice of merging government and party power at the highest levels of the two hierarchies was adopted. The incumbent prime minister was elected party general secretary. Soon after, however, a decision was made to separate the party and the government so that the party could function better as a watchdog over government performance. When the separation proved susceptible to the promotion of competition between the two, the party secretariat and premiership were combined once again.

Similar confusion prevailed with regard to the relationship between the party and the parliament. Having won total control of the parliament, the party could not resolve the matter of its ties with the legislative branch of the government. The trilateral relations among the party, the government, and the parliament continued to plague the new system until the summer of 1978, when the forces of revolution swept the party into oblivion.

Related matters of encouragement and containment of competition within the exclusive party presented even more confusion. As noted earlier, one reason for the formation of the new party was to provide a mechanism of articulation of interest for which rewards from the system could be demanded. Given the plurality of interest and the abundance of rewards available to the regime, it was apparent that considerable competition would develop among groups expecting favorable treatment by the regime.

It was unclear whether the triad of government, party, and parliament should be utilized to channel this competition or whether the party as the broadest of the three should be entrusted with this task. The first choice could risk closer identification of the public interest with any one of these three institutions and engender the renewal of genuine parliamentary opposition. What if the disgruntled public, unhappy with its share of the rewards, identified fully with the parliament and sought to impose policies which the government could not espouse? Would not the next logical step be the removal of a government unwilling or unable to submit to a parliament representing disaffected groups?

That the risk of such a transformation would ultimately subject the government to accountability to the parliament, (even though both were controlled by the same party), was not lost upon the Shah. For if the executive could be made accountable to the parliament, there was no assurance that the Shah's supreme authority would not become the target of such restriction later.

Interestingly enough, some theorists within the party hierarchy believed that precisely the same process should be allowed to occur. They believed the party should become a mechanism for developing a limited parliamentary system in which the party would ultimately link the executive with the legislature. Because the supreme authority retained its constitutional power of dissolution and veto of legislation, the prospect of an effective challenge to the royal authority was considered remote.[6]

The views of these theorists did not prevail. The single party itself introduced the notion of ideological wings — one

11

named constructive, the other progressive. These wings, which were neither ideological nor personal, were assigned the task of channeling competition within the party. Though each rallied around a well-known personality already represented in government and the party leadership, they were not allowed to operate as centers of even limited autonomous power. Nor were they invested with an ideology, since the one party had already accepted the three principles of Monarchy, Constitution, and the White Revolution. The functions of these wings remained unclear throughout their existence.

Some party members believed that the wings could help implement the concept of democratic centralism. That is to say, in the curse of discussing policy and decisions, the two wings might facilitate the presentation of various and even diametrically opposed solutions. Once the majority reached a decision, it would, of course, be binding on the entire party. Other members stressed the need for containing competition within the party, insofar as distribution of rewards was concerned. As such, they felt these wings should be affiliated with parliamentary groups as well as with various ministries and business institutions.

Could this arrangement in turn revive the former government-controlled two-party system? The prospect was not entirely unwelcome. Indeed, a year before the demise of the party, some members had been thinking along those lines. One of its leaders told this writer that just as had been the case for Turkey in 1950, so could a single Iranian party encourage a transition to a two- or even a multi-party system, once the "historical mission" of Rastakhiz had been fulfilled.[7]

It appeared that some theorists believed that the "historical mission" of Rastakhiz was political education and mobilization and that once these were accomplished, a dogmatic attachment to the concept of one party would become unnecessary. If the regime had survived the revolutionary challenge of 1978-79, it is likely that Rastakhiz would have been allowed to disintegrate prior to the June parliamentary election, in the hope that one of the two wings would retain a majority. In apparent preparation for this eventuality some party members cited parliamentary elections in Mexico and Singapore as examples of one-party systems in which the government party has emerged as the ruling party in successive elections, while generally tolerating free participation of opposition parties.[8]

Altered socio-economic conditions and four years of involvement in political education apparently invalidated the previously plausible argument in favor of a one-party system. But was it possible to return to pre-1975 conditions? Once again the prospect of parliamentary elections forced the regime to take a hand in resolving disputes within the political party. These disputes could have been resolved in various ways.

a) The regime could have abandoned the notion of the party as a mechanism of political participation and utilized it merely as a means for conducting the parliamentary elections.

b) It could have reinstated a genuine two-party system which would have allowed legitimate parliamentary opposition to function. Either a new group of pro-regime intellectuals known as a "group to study Iran's problems in the wake of the Shah-people revolution," or one or the other existing wings could have performed that task.

c) The government could have permitted the formation of a multi-party system which would participate in the general elections and hope that a workable coalition of pro-government parties would emerge.

On the anniversary of the adoption of the Constitution in

13

carly August the Shah chose the latter option and pledged that all political parties except the illegal Communist party would be free to participate in the upcoming election.[9] That pledge effectively ended the era of the one-party system. Once more, the impending constitutionally mandated election for the new Majlis forced the regime to make a decision concerning participation in the political process. Just as in 1975 when the impending June election forced the Shah to choose a one-party system, now the upcoming election compelled him to sanction a new formula.

The inability of the regime to resolve the issues of the scope and limits of political participation under an authoritarian regime played significant role in the collapse of the government in the ensuing months. A major component of the revolutionary upheaval of 1978-79 was the widespread awareness of the lack of participation in a country which was rapidly modernizing in other areas.

Increased literacy, enhanced media exposure and the mass exodus of the peasantry from the countryside to the cities all combined to produce a profound need for the expression of opinion and the demand for a voice in the affairs of state. These desires could not be satisfied by an imposed mass interest group like the new party. The party could promote material interest and bestow economic reward. But it could not satisfy political demands including those bringing into question the concentration of political authority in one center and indeed in one person.

The failure of this experiment with a one-party system once again revealed that genuine political parties in Iran commonly flourish only in opposition and in conditions of relative political freedom. In cases in which monolithic parties have been successful in controlling power, that control has usually been less than total or has been held for only a brief period.

Review of past examples of regime-sponsored political parties certainly supports these observations. One such case is the formation of Iran's Democratic party "Hezbe Demokrate Iran," by Ahmad Ghavam in the spring of 1946.[10] This government party was created as a shrewd political measure to win the election of the 15th Majlis, a parliament of which the makeup was particularly crucial, since it was to consider a Soviet-Iranian oil agreement. Since the party was one of several which contested that election, the situation was quite different from the 1975 experience. Furthermore, this party operated in the context of a parliamentary system in which at least three centers of power coexisted. These were the government, the parliament, and the Shah, none of which enjoyed authority that approached the absolute concentration of the Shah's between 1963 and 1978.

Nonetheless, the party used similar techniques to mobilize civil servants and peasants and secured nearly unanimous control of the Majlis in 1947. Once the Majlis rejected the Soviet-Iranian oil agreement, it was only a matter of time before the party and its leaders disappeared from the scene.

Several years later (1952), the National Front represented the pro-Mossadegh movement which contested the election to the 17th Majlis. Mossadegh, unlike Ghavam and later the Shah, did not fully sponsor a party. Instead, the Front consisted of a coalition of four groups. The coalition did not win a reliable majority in the Majlis and Mossadegh dissolved the parliament at the end of his tenure in July 1953.[11]

Although both Mossadegh and Ghavam used government resources to mobilize and organize political parties, the Shah outdid them both for several reasons. Financial resources available to the regime in 1975 were by far richer and more numerous. Socio-economic change in the intervening 25 years had expanded those elements of the population which could be mobilized. The Iranian state apparatus was in a position to utilize modern techniques of mass communication and propaganda, some borrowed from totalitarian regimes.

None of these advantages, however, achieved the desired objective of cementing bonds of affinity between the politically significant members of the population and the regime. Instead, the imposed party became another symbol of the regime's oppression and a cause of the growing alienation of that group of Iranians.

Without a doubt the growing alienation of important segments of society was also due to reasons other than their inability to participate politically in the Iranian system. For the intelligentsia and the professional groups the alienation was fundamentally political and only marginally economic. For the lower middle class, the newly urbanized peasantry and more significantly, for the bazaari and the clergy, the alienation from the regime had diverse and at times contradictory causes.

One student of Iranian politics cites the repercussion of the credit crunch which came at the end of 1976 and the beginning of 1977 as a major cause of popular grievances. This credit squeeze affected the booming building industry which had absorbed tens of thousands of unskilled workers from the countryside and which could no longer employ them, thus adding to the ranks of *lumpenprolaterliat*. [12]

But even before the credit crunch these thousands of unskilled workers who, enticed by higher wages, had left their villages or had refused to return home after their two-year military service experienced considerable social dislocation. In Isfahan alone many of the over 300,000 rural migrants lived away from their families and crowded in slums. Though earning relatively high wages, the galloping inflation had turned them into the urban poor.

As for the intelligentsia, their alienation was primarily political. One of their representatives, an American-educated professor of economics wrote: "Young professionals want to escape the establishment, which is everybody who has real power. Morally and financially this establishment is corrupt. We are not brave enough to join the opposition but by being at the University we maintain a passive opposition."[13]

In an eloquent condemnation of the regime, he added, "Our case against the government is lack of freedom; all creativity has been crushed. As an economist I cannot talk about malnutrition or underdevelopment. A whole generation has been raised, educated and given no freedom; ninety percent of the people have been left out of the development."[14]

In the same vein another intellectual who was at least temporarily coopted by the regime declared, "The great problem is lack of freedom. We have lots of intellectuals and technocrats who have views, but they are never allowed to express them. Everything is dictated from the top. We have an intelligentsia but they have no chance to participate. They are just supposed to support the regime. They don't like slavishly supporting the Shah, so they turn against him."[15]

Another grievance of the intelligentsia was the system of justice. For years the civil court system was completely controlled by the Shah, who appointed all judges at the recommendation of the prime minister. Even so, judicial responsibilities often shifted from civil courts to military tribunals.

Numerically the Iranian intelligentsia is one of the largest in the Middle East. Government statistics indicate that it increased from 6 percent of the total population employed in 1956 to 13 percent in 1976. When merchants and businessmen are included, the total is about 25 percent.[16]

Apart from political alienation from the regime, the intelligentsia share with most of the population a common religious background which in time of crisis could be utilized

17

by the clergy to mobilize the masses for political action. An examination of the interaction between the clergy and the lower middle class and the bazaar merchants and tradesmen during this revolutionary upheaval will demonstrate just how susceptible all these groups were to this type of mobilization.

2

The Religious Dimension

The exact role of the Shia clergy in this revolution remains and will remain a matter of intense speculative interest.[17]

The Shiites trace their heritage to Ali, the cousin and son-in-law of the prophet Mohammad. The descendants of Ali represent a chain of charismatic leaders known as Imam, the Twelfth of whom went into occulation in 940 A. D. Mojtaheds or Mojtahedin, the Shia leaders, are representatives of this last Imam. Once Iran adopted Twelve Shiism in 1501 as the state religion, the positions of the Mojtaheds assumed a political significance which compelled the secular Shahs to accommodate them.[18]

The relations of the two Pahlavi shahs with the Mojtahedin have been mixed, ranging from an uneasy coexistence to the subservience of one to the other. Since at least the early 1960's when some of the most powerful Mojtaheds denounced the proposed land reform laws, the clergy as a whole has become estranged from the regime.[19]

That the Shia leaders progressively assumed the main

burden of mobilizing the masses of their followers is indisputable. In effect, the revolution acquired a populist characteristic once the Shia religion could be utilized to rally all opponents of the regime around such popular symbols as an anti-oppression crusade.

The successful utilization of the masses' religion as well as the increasing radicalization of the religious forces may be attributed initially to the repressive policies of the regime. As indicated earlier, the regime suppressed other outlets of freedom — the press, political parties, student organizations, and any forum for free speech — leaving dissidents little choice but to organize behind religion. Obviously, the large network of approximately 80,000 mosques and holy shrines served by about 180,000 mullahs facilitated this process of gravitation toward religion.

Two other factors further enhanced the attraction of the Shia religion to the alienated. One factor was the relative ease with which the mullahs could be anti-government in their sermons, couching these in religious metaphors. Second, the Shia religion was traditionally anti-authority, having been founded in opposition to Caliphs who took command of Islam after the death of the prophet.

Thus the security apparatus of the regime found it difficult to level charges of anti-state activism in dealing with normal activities of the mosques. "In spite of the power of the security forces, the mosques and religious centers were sanctuaries where we met, talked, prepared, organized and grew," acknowledged the secular leader of Iran's Liberation Movement at the height of the revolutionary turmoil in October, 1978.[20]

In a sense this was a religious revival only in form and not in substance. That is to say, alienation and opposition to the regime for political rather than primarily moral and religious reasons motivated the population. Moreover, the mullahs were not merely reflecting popular opinion when they denounced the regime. Many of them had compelling personal grievances such as the land reform which had reduced the "Oghaf" shrine-controlled land or certain judicial modernization measures which reduced their functions in marriage, divorce, and other family matters.[21] No doubt their disaffection was further aggravated by the regime's portrayal of them as ignorant, backward reactionaries who opposed modernization programs out of selfish interest.

Control of the school system was yet another area in which the power of the Shia hierarchy had been eroded. Although the clergy had not totally controlled it in the recent past, nonetheless the school system represented substantial means for religious education and mobilization. Once the clergy lost control of regular schools to the state, the remaining religious schools of Madresseh became even more integrated as centers of anti-regime activities. According to one observer, the city of Qom in 1976 had acquired "an atmosphere of siege and courageous passive hostility to a state perceived to be the stronger but morally corrupt opponent."[22]

It is important to note that apart from progressively adamant opposition to the regime, the religious leadership did not present a homogeneous force. On the question of the degree of politicization of the clergy or indeed the advisability or nature of revolutionary pressure against the regime, great variation in opinions existed.

At the moderate center of the spectrum stood Ayattolah Mohammad Kazem Shariatmadari, who from his headquarters at Qom made frequent pronouncements on the revival of Shia as a political force. Acknowledging that religion used to be considered marginal — separate from the mainstream of events — he attributed its revival as a potent political force to its ability to answer problems of conscience.

"It provides a vantage point for fighting injustice. In our Shia religion spiritual leaders are ready at all times to assert the truth and the right."[23]

This was equally true of the temporal as well as the spiritual sphere. Justice and injustice were described in a political context. "We have never had free elections. The elections in the past were all dominated by local magnates or consultates of foreign power. It was not right to locate authority to marry in the civil officials, for marriage was not a deal or contract but something spiritual and so it should be performed by religious authorities."[24]

Even a cursory review of his rebuttal to the regime's accusation that religious leaders were anti-progressive, reactionary, and anachronistic demonstrates the clergy's awareness of the need for broadening its appeal. "We want science, technology, and educated men and women, physicians, surgeons, engineers. But we also want clean and honest political leaders. Those who make the charges against us are themselves reactionary, because their goal is to stop us from instituting a government of hope. The Government of God is the government of the people by the people."[25]

Political moderation may have been dictated by the same consideration. At least until late October 1978 his specific request was for a return to the 1906 Constitution, with a Supreme Council of five religious leaders who have a veto right over all laws. "If they found the laws repugnant to Islam or to principles of Justice or against the interests of the majority, they could reject them."[26]

These demands of Shariatmadari and his supporters were far from radical. As a group, they were willing to negotiate a solution to the problem if a fair and just government and parliament could emerge from a free election.

Their moderation was either misinterpreted or not taken advantage of by the regime, which continued to view

Shariatmadari as non-political and "afraid to speak out for the regime because the government offered him no protection."[27] This failure, in turn, contributed to the radicalization of the moderate faction of the clergy by the end of 1978.

Although over the last 25 years some important members of the Shia clergy remained non-political and on occasion even supportive of the regime, it is also true that a number of those who became politicized gradually acquired leadership in the movement.

Most persistent among these critics was Ayatollah Ruhollah Khomeini, whose condemnation of the Shah prior to and during the June 1963 religious riots caused his exile, first to Turkey and then to Iraq. Khomeini saw politics as the logical extension of the Shia religion. Persistently and skillfully he won over to his viewpoint several prominent Shia leaders inside the country, and as the protest movement gathered momentum, more of his fellow Ayatollahs publicly challenged the regime.

Among the more outspoken leaders was Ayatollah Mahmoud Taleghani who spent five years in prison. He played an active role in the final stages of the revolution, once he was released from prison as a belated gesture of appeasement on the part of the regime toward the opposition.

Although Khomeini gradually came to symbolize the unity of purpose of the revolutionary coalition, both Shariatmadari and Taleghani also played important roles. Shariatmadari used his vast reputation as a pious religious scholar to convince his followers of the logic of political action and its justification on religious grounds. Taleghani, who had very close ties with the National Front and the honor of suffering at the hands of a repressive regime, contributed to keeping intact the secular and religious alliance. Numerous other lesser known provincial Shia leaders also became political activists once Shariatmadari from Qom and Khomeini from foreign exile sanctioned and, indeed, required participation in the revolutionary movement.

Apart from the top Shia leaders, pronounced radicalism had penetrated the ranks of younger and more politicized Iranians, particularly the new generation of theological students. One student of Iranian politics, seeing some parallel with the revolutionary priests of Latin America or the Christian Marxists of the West believes that current Shia radicalism grew in part as a result of widespread disillusionment with either Western reformism or Soviet Marxism.[28] The former ideology came to be judged as inapplicable to the conditions of the viciously class-ridden Iranian society, while the latter suffered from identification with Soviet foreign policy which had betrayed the interests of the Iranian people more than once since 1921.

Shia clergy had long espoused the doctrine of a just social change, as evidenced by their active participation in the 1906 constitutional movement and in the struggle for oil national-ization of the early 1950's. In the 1960's the radical Shias were organized either in the underground party of Iran's Liberation Movement or in the more extreme guerrilla move-ment of the Mojahedine Khalghe Iran (Crusaders of Iranian People), which was dedicated to the violent overthrow of the regime.

A well-known theoretician of radical Shiism was the late Ali Shariati, whose numerous writings in and outside Iran appealed strongly to the younger and Western-educated Iranians. According to his socio-economic interpretation, a true Islamic society required as a precondition an equitable system of production and distribution.

Shariati interpreted Shia thought as a historic ideology of the oppressed and regarded radical socio-political action as the ultimate proof of faith. He portrayed Shia martyrs as revolutionary heroes to be emulated by contemporary activists.

Other spokesmen for the radical Shia have endeavored to give a progressive image to their movement. Denying that theirs is an anti-Western ideology, they have declared that what they found offensive in the West is the obsession with materialism and its various forms of colonialism and imperialism. The radical Shia are receptive to the progressive and universalistic aspects of Western civilization. One wrote, "Islamic civilization and Western civilization can and should merge in order to create a better civilization for all."[29]

3

The Politicization of the Bazaar

Although a radical interpretation of Shiaism appealed to the younger generation of Iranians, including university students and high school teachers, and helped strengthen their revolutionary efforts, the group which more significantly broadened the basis of anti-regime opposition was the *bazaari*. The instruments of their mobilization was also the Shia religion.

There are three principal reasons for the susceptibility of the *bazaari* to mobilization efforts of the clergy. First, they have been traditional allies of the mullahs and for centuries the two have been mutually dependent. Until the state took over the schools the mullahs were responsible for educating the children of the *bazaari,* who in turn financed the clergy and their diverse charity organizations, such as hospitals and orphanages. Even today the *bazaari* finance the network of Islamic schools, most of the budget for five theological colleges, and up to 80 percent of the support for all clergy.

Second, the *bazaari* could organize crowds for demonstrations, almost instantly. They have traditionally performed the role of appointing leaders for three major "processions" in the Islamic calendar, the foremost being the Ashura.[30] In Tehran alone, one report estimated the number of procession leaders or "contactmen" who could be summoned on short notice at 5,000.[31] That their expertise in crowd mobilization could lend itself just as easily to non-religious demonstrations was proven both in the early 1950's and during the current revolution. In doing so the *bazaari* could rely on another segment of the population, namely the rural inhabitants. Traditionally, by means of the purchase of agricultural surplus and the sale of consumer goods, the *bazaari* had maintained close ties with the peasantry.

The third reason for the susceptibility of the *bazaari* has been their own sense of alienation. In the last 20 years their economic power has plummeted, with the state taking over more than 80 percent of the GNP. Their nouveau riche bureaucratic successors were westernized and newcomers to the political scene. Even though the *bazaari* benefited from the oil boom after 1973, once their status declined, their hostility toward the regime was revived.

The general decline in the economic strength of the *bazaari* may be attributed to:

a) Huge government-owned industrial units which sprang up throughout the country over the 15 years, 1963-78.

b) Increased involvement and near monopoly of the state in export-import businesses.

c) Expansion of the banking system which first rivaled and then pre-empted the credit institutions of the *bazaari.*

d) Breakdown of traditional patterns of socio-economic organization which served to accentuate the opposition of the *bazaari* to what was vaguely termed "modernization."

Notwithstanding the adverse effects of this "modernization," that same process did expand the opportunities for education and to some extent mobility for the children of the *bazaari.* One report indicates that at the present time

28

members of *bazaari* families constitute the majority of university teachers, tradesmen, lawyers, journalists, technocrats and the middle cadres of the services and the armed forces, and that the present situation is unlikely to change for at least another decade.[32]

The *bazaari* are organized in an informal and loosely institutionalized pattern. Active *bazaari* are organized in a number of missions called "Heyat," each in charge of hundreds of religious gathering places other than mosques. These groups supplement and complement the functions of mullahs through the following types of religious centers:

1) Tekyeh, which is used for 40 days, starting with the first of Moharram, the month of martyrdom of Imam Hossein and ending in Arbain which formally terminates the mourning period

2) Hosseiniyeh, which in addition to the above center, is used for incidental religious gatherings such as mourning for the dead

3) Mahdiyeh, named in honor of the missing Imam and often used for religious instruction or recital of the Qoran

4) Taaziyeh or Shia religious passion plays, staged most solemnly on the occasion of the death of Imam Hossein on Moharram 10. These plays could take place in any of the above sites.[33]

Intimately connected with the "Heyats" managing these centers are literally thousands of pilgrimage organizers who take the faithful on group tours to holy places and who exercise considerable influence among Moslems during the Haj season.

Leaders of the groups are never elected but are easily recognizable in every trade by their reputation for piety, wisdom, and age. Their means of enforcement is social ostracism rather than formal coercive instruments of excommunication or boycott. Their refusal to endorse fellow *bazaari* as upright and good men would result in their social rejection and inevitable business reverses. This informal leadership structure has not rendered the *bazaari* socially incohesive. Largely as a result of intermarriage and parochial association, they have managed to maintain an impressive degree of solidarity.

Another criterion for groupings among *bazaari* is family and provincial background. In the capital city larger provincial groups like the Azarbayjanis may have their own Tekyeh or mosque through which they maintain close and effective links with the *bazaari* in their home towns.

Although the record of political activity of the *bazaari* is a mixed one, it is safe to say that they have seldom openly supported any government seen as basically westerized and diametrically opposed to their deeply traditional values and conservative institutions. They have resented state intervention on the grounds that their own business community had adequate corrective safeguards. With increased government tendencies toward "etatism" backed by oil wealth, it was obvious that the state and the *bazaari* were destined to collide.

The seeds for confrontation were sown late in 1974 by the inauguration of a seemingly well-intentioned anti-profiteering campaign. By early summer 1978 the campaign had to be abandoned, as the storms of protest gathered strength in Iran's political climate.

That anti-profiteering campaign had evolved around several phases:

1) First guild chambers were legislated into existence. Patterned after the Western model, they sought to replace the traditional leadership and organizational structure of the *bazaari*.

2) Once they were created, the guilds assumed the function of political-commercial control.

3) Approximately 10,000 recruits from all walks of life — students, teachers, housewives — were unleashed upon the bazaars, with the right to "hand out fines and recommend stiff penalties which ranged from prison to deportation and closure of place of business."[34]

Government statistics show that in the first ten months of its operations the Guild Courts fined or closed down more than 250,000 business units in Tehran; sent 8,000 merchants to jail for 2 months to 3 years, and deported another 23,000 shopkeepers for 3 months to 5 years. When the campaign came to a halt in late August there were 150,000 suits still pending in the special Guild Courts.

Another anti-*bazaari* measure was the Tehran municipality's plan to build an eight-lane freeway through the center of the main bazaar. In addition, there was to be a general ban on repairs and building in the neighborhood and periphery of the bazaar.

Simultaneously, the Ministry of Health started a campaign to extend the program of social security to all *bazaari.* It required that the Ministry be notified of the number of employees and that both full time and temporary employees, many of whom were students, be covered by social insurance. These measures intensified the hostility of the *bazaari* toward the government, which was accused by some of them of ". . .making us the whipping boys of Iran to create a smoke screen for the vast corruption that was going on in the government and in the bosom of the royal family."[35] Having no political party and no interest group where they could air their grievances, the *bazaari* took them to the mosques and their traditional allies, the mullahs.

A further unintended result of the anti-profiteering campaign was its impact as a sort of school for mobilization and agitation in which the participants had little difficulty in shifting their attention from their fellow lower middle-class countrymen to the regime itself.[36]

The above evidence illustrates the close interaction between the *bazaari* and the mullahs. Which was the more dominant in this interaction is not entirely clear. However, one astute observer of Iranian politics has cited the following reasons for his belief that politically it was the *bazaari* who influenced the Shia clergy.

"a) In addition to holding the purse strings, the Bazaar has all the network of information and mobilization.

b) It could do something concrete and tangible by closing down. Even in a situation of decline in its economic power, such a procedure is bound to be effective.

c) Denied the active support of the *bazaari,* the mullahs could not sustain a prolonged political campaign — as evidenced by a fairly tranquil period of about 15 years."[37]

During the revolutionary turmoil the cooperation between the two assumed such a high degree of coordination and intensity that the issue of their relative strength became academic. Nonetheless, the Iranian experience of the recent past shows that neither alone nor together could the *bazaari* and the Shia clergy unleash revolutionary forces. It has been only in league with other social groups — the intelligentsia, the working class, and even some sectors of the military — that twice within this generation the *bazaari* have played a crucial political role.

While specific economic causes of the disaffection of the *bazaari* must be noted, the general mismanagement of Iran's economic structure over the last two decades merits closer scrutiny. Two important considerations should be recognized. The first is that mere availability of vast financial resources could not generate political stability. The second is that misjudgments in the allocation of resources and determination of priorities in a planned economy can produce uncontrollable political consequences.

4

Economic Mismanagement

Both independent and government-sponsored studies of Iran's economic development in this period agree on certain outcomes such as the growth rate, increase in income per capita, the GNP, and GNP per capita.[38]. What is not generally agreed upon is whether a series of five-year economic plans had brought about a more egalitarian distribution of the national income.

Similarly, although the land reform did succeed in granting ownership of land to a large segment of the peasantry, it is not possible to determine whether the net result was a perceptible increase in the buying power of the peasants or a larger share of national income accruing to the recently propertied farmers. Furthermore, the land reform was not accompanied by the dispensation of credits, fertilizer, tractors, and improvement of irrigation facilities that modern farming requires. In short, many of the functions which traditionally had been performed by the now dispossessed landlords were not assumed on any large scale by the government-sponsored cooperatives.

Perhaps the most dramatic evidence of the failure of land reform to improve the lot of the peasants is in their great exodus to the cities, particularly in the 1973-76 period of the great construction boom.

Politically, the failure of land reform was equally significant. As in a number of European countries, the landed peasantry could have become the cornerstone of new political parties. Indeed, the architect of the land reform, the late Dr. Hassan Arsanjani, had asked the Shah for permission to form a party to be known as "Khordeh Malekin" (small holders). Fearing that the great popularity of his minister of agriculture would be institutionalized in an uncontrollable fashion, the Shah refused to allow such a development.[39] Instead, the peasants were mobilized either to join the one-party system in 1975 or to attend various congresses and political rallies which could be controlled easily and never institutionalized.

The peasantry was, therefore, as alienated from the political system as were other social groups. The regime was to find that mere land ownership did not generate the kind of political gratitude that could be counted upon in a situation of crisis.

Consequently, the regime's experience in land reform provided still another indication of its failure to complement socio-economic change with commensurate political change.

An equally significant consideration is the scope of economic disparity which existed among important segments of society. Despite differences in the particular measurement techniques, the findings were all similar. They showed that while the national wealth was increasing, many people, particularly in the countryside, were relatively worse off than before. One report of the Plan and Budget Organization indicated that the income share of the top 20 percent of urban Iranians had risen from 57.5 percent in 1972 to 63.5 percent in 1975. The share of the middle 40 percent had dropped from 31 to 25.3 percent, and the share of the bottom 40 percent had declined from 11.5 to 11 percent. Whereas urban consumption per capita was about twice as high as that in the rural area in 1959, by 1972 it was three times greater.[40]

Another method is the measurement of the inequality of income among individuals, families or classes by drawing the so-called Lorenzo curve. The curve results from measuring percentages of the population along the horizontal axis and those of income along the vertical one. If each percent of the population had exactly the same percent of income, the curve of distribution would be a straight line, coinciding with the diagonal. The more bent the Lorenzo curve, the larger the area between it and the diagonal and the greater the socio-economic inequality. Consecutive measurements taken of countries which are moving toward greater equality show that the curve will flatten and the area of inequality will shrink. The area between the Lorenzo curve and the diagonal permits the calculation of a single number called the Gini index. This index is a summary measure of the extent of socio-economic inequality prevailing in a country.[41]

When this measure is applied to Iran in the period 1971-75, we find that the curve of inequality has become more bent, thereby producing a larger area between itself and a diagonal line. Stated differently, both the percentage of the poorest and the richest have increased, leading to a further condition of alienation of a large segment of the population.

Neither land reform, which promised substantially better living conditions for the rural population, nor economic manipulation designed to generate a more equitable distribution of national wealth convinced the lower and middle classes that their share from the burgeoning oil revenue was fair and equitable. Parenthetically, the failures in economic development in Iran provided striking evidence against the facile assumption that the burden of massive, grinding poverty in developing countries would be removed automatically by economic growth and social modernization.

It is true that per capita income in most developing countries has grown more rapidly than ever, but so have unemployment, malnutrition, abject poverty, and hunger. Within such developing countries as Iran and India the income gap between the richest and poorest members of society has increased. In Iran we have seen how this income gap produced acute political strains that contributed in large measure to the unleashing of revolutionary forces.

Undoubtedly the desire for rapid modernization compounded the problem for Iran. The regime had sought to condense the developmental process to a generation or two, whereas the advanced nations had taken centuries to transform themselves from agricultural to industrial societies. In implementing its plans for modernization, the government failed to combine policies of accelerated growth with measures to assure that the relative income of the poorest segment of the population would not deteriorate.

According to one recent study, in a number of developing countries the undesirable trade-off of rapid development has been avoided.[42] Even a cursory analysis of the examples of Israel, Japan, South Korea, Singapore, and Taiwan goes a long way to explain the Iranian failure.

This study identifies several phases in the successful development of these countries:

1) Redistribution of assets which focused primarily on land but also imposed some curbs on the use and accumulation of financial capital in order to avoid excessive centralization in industry and political power. In the Iranian case, while land reform sought to accomplish this type of redistribution, no significant measures were taken to curb private and public growth of finance capital. In fact, quite the reverse was true.

The state consciously sought further concentration of industrial and economic power.

2) Improvement in agricultural productivity in order to generate an economic surplus for the accumulation of industrial capital and the release of the labor force needed for industrialization. During the period from 1963 to 1976, agricultural productivity declined rapidly and whatever labor force was released for industrialization was not the result of any economic surplus but rather of more attractive working conditions in urban areas. Desperate attempts to reverse this situation came too late and once the credit crunch slowed down the construction industry in major cities, the masses of unskilled laborers could not return to rural areas in a productive capacity.

3) Massive improvement in human capital, especially by raising the level of literacy and skills of the population. Although the Iranian regime's attempt was somewhat successful, its results were not commensurate with the rapid population growth over the last decades. The literacy corps and the increase in opportunities for primary education managed to raise the level of literacy from about 18 to nearly 50 percent in 25 years. But in the area of trade and technical training, the record of the government is dismal.

4) The final stage of a rational development policy required concentrated growth in labor-intensive industries. In larger countries industrialization could be oriented toward satisfying domestic demands, particularly when there was technology to replace imports. Iran is a relatively large developing nation and the regime was evidently conscious of the need to satisfy these demands. But while the economy moved rapidly toward consumerism, it did not succeed in constructing a sufficient technological foundation to replace imports. Instead, vast sums of oil revenue were allocated to importing consumer goods including foodstuffs in which

merely seven years ago Iran had been fully self-sufficient.

In retrospect then, it is clear that the growth strategy was ill-conceived. Neglect of agricultural development and haste to satisfy consumer appetites as a sort of political tranquilizer simply aggravated social tensions. But even a correct growth strategy could not insure the genuine stability of the regime.

When by the summer of 1978 the forces of opposition had coalesced, economic grievances were not among the major reasons causing the dissidents' espousal of radical political goals. Initially their objective was a return to genuine constitutional government but in the end it was the overthrow of the monarchical regime.

Many who had prospered materially under the regime saw nothing contradictory in attempting to bring it down, once they became convinced it could not be reformed. Other individuals whose political apathy literally had been bought responded to the Biblical admonition that "man does not live by bread alone." For them the moral imperative dictated that material loss or even deprivation was not too high a price to pay for political freedom and dignity.

5

Challenging the System

Recent Iranian history abounds with examples of interaction between political alienation and opposition to the
established authority. One pioneering study has shown how
there may be both negative and positive forms of challenge to
the established political order, depending on the degree of
alienation and the goals of the challengers. In a most extreme
form a negative challenge is manifested by membership in a
subversive conspiracy for the purpose of forcibly deposing
the regime.[43]

In recent postware Iran various extreme ideologies, from
communism to Islamic fundamentalism, were most
responsive to the need of this type of system challenge. In the
1941-53 era the communist movement in particular enjoyed
almost a monopoly as a vehicle for both negative and positive
challenge to the Iranian system.

This writer's study of the communist movement has
confirmed the strong attraction of this function of communist ideology for those politically articulate Iranians who
have been estranged from the system.[44] For them the com-

munist movement provided a channel for at least a negative challenge to the social and political system. By joining a party dedicated to overthrowing the regime in power, the participants satisfied the most extreme form of this type of challenge. They could also use its less extreme form of passive resistance, such as refusal to vote, denial of labor and other modes of protest in which the alienation toward the regime is not overtly displayed, for fear of retribution.

In the present upheaval we witness the emergence of a number of other extreme ideologies that competed with communism as a vehicle of negative challenge to the Iranian regime. We can also observe how the milder form of protest, positive challenge, became widespread, and finally, how a combination of both these forms succeeded in overthrowing the Iranian system.

With the discrediting of the pro-Soviet communist party that resulted from the ideological disarray of the post-Stalin era and the severe repression used by the reinstated regime of the Shah, by the late 1960's several additional radical factions had emerged. These groups, which had waged guerrilla warfare in Iran for about a decade, surfaced during the 1978-79 upheaval and they are likely to continue their efforts for radicalization of the Iranian revolution in the coming years.

The political and ideological orientation of these groups can be identified according to their positions left of center in the political spectrum. The center, which coalesced around Khomeini, is a phenomenon of recent origin and represents a merger of secular and religious anti-regime forces. The following groups exist to the left of this faction:

1) Iran's Liberation Movement, though secular has deep ties with Shia clergy. It is an offshoot of the National Front movement and was formed by Mehdi Bazargan at the height of the repression. Even when the Shah initiated some measure of liberalization in the last year of his rule, this faction never

received the sanction of legitimacy. This group may be described as a secular-puritanical movement which tried to combine modern Western modes of technology and government with highly moral and puritanic concepts of Islam.

2) Formed in the fall of 1978, the Socalist Workers Party of Iran belongs to the left of Iran's Liberation Movement and is dedicated to bringing about a non-Soviet socialist revolution in Iran. Led by a group of recently returned political exiles, such as Dr. Reza Barahani from the United States, this party seeks the ultimate formation of a Peasants-Workers Republic with freedom and equal rights for men and women. It also demands the restoration of Revolutionary Constitutional Societies, which functioned as a parallel government in the early years of the Constitutional Revolution in the 1906-1911 era.[45]

3) To its left is the Islamic Crusaders of Iranian People (Mojahedine Khalghe Iran) which was the main non-Marxist guerrilla group which had been active in urban warfare against the regime since about 1966. Their ideological goal is the establishment of an Islamic but egalitarian republic which is occasionally characterized by the term "Eshteraki Islam" or Islamic socialism.

4) Within the membership of the above group were those with a Marxist bent who later formed the "Struggle for Freedom" and demanded a peoples' democratic republic via armed action and large-scale recruitment. In the Iranian media they are known as Marxist Mojahedin.

Together the latter two groups suffered at least 57 deaths, either in the course of armed skirmishes or by firing squads. An examination of a list of 51 of its martyrs reveals that nearly 65 percent were either university students or recent graduates in such fields as engineering, medicine, business, and accounting and that 15 percent of them were women.[46]

5) The other main urban guerrilla group, called The

41

Organization of Devoted People's Guerrillas (Sazemane Cherikhaye Fedayee Khalgh) regards the Mojahedin as a useful staging post from religious to secular socialism.

The ODPG has been involved in numerous acts of violence against the security forces, starting with a suicidal attack on the Gendarmerie garrison in Siyahkal in the Mazanderan jungles in the spring of 1971. As a result of either skirmishes with security forces or conviction by military tribunals, the entire organization has lost about 155 members. Of these nearly 50 percent were students, 30 percent government and other office workers, and 20 percent engineers, workers, and others. A total of 12 percent were women.[47]

In the final stage of the revolutionary takeover this group showed signs of concern about the direction of the revolution and the predominance of religious leadership. One of its proposals was that the emerging Revolutionary Council include representatives of the millions of striking workers, particularly those in the oil industry. Once the triumph of the revolution seemed imminent, the ODPG disassociated itself from the Islamic identity of the revolution by stating that "the revolution is not in the monopoly of any one particular group, rather it is a liberating and anti-imperialistic upheaval to herald a free and democratic Iran."[48]

This group called the Fedayin in popular press is an umbrella organization that integrates several leftist groups with a long history of radical political activity in Iran. Three of these are:

a) the pro-Tudeh group whose main claim to revolutionary reputation is its long and persistent opposition to the Shah. The group de-emphasized its pro-Soviet ties, claiming that the Tudeh is no different from Euro-Communism. Moreover, it asserted that the Sino-Soviet rivalry had given the Soviets the edge, since China had much closer ties with the Shah than did the Soviet Union.

b) the Jazani group, named after Bijan Jazani, a victim of guerrilla war with the security forces, which concentrates on political activity and education.

c) the third group which did not abandon armed uprising was also named after fallen guerrillas, the Ahmad Zade-Pooyan. Both of the latter two groups believed that a multiparty democratic republic with respect for all religions and self-determination for ethnic groups was attainable and desirable.[49]

As to the formal position of the exiled leadership of the Tudeh party, there is considerable evidence indicative of their lack of preparation for massive mobilization of the Iranian movement and their traditional hostility toward movements in whose formation they have had little or no part.

The old leadership of the party communicated its view in a new underground publication, *Novid*. One lead article entitled, "The Tudeh Party and the Moslem Movement" volunteered the party's readiness to "put at the disposal of our friends from other political groups all our political propaganda and technical resources for the campaign against the Shah." The secretary general of the party, Iraj Eskandari, was on record as saying that "As far as the religious aspect of the present movement is concerned, it should be emphasized that the Shiite clergy cannot be viewed as a force demanding a return to the past or the Middle Ages. To a significant extent the position of the clergy reflects popular feelings. And the fact that the religious movement is now playing an important role in the mobilization of democratic nationalist forces against the dictatorial anti-nationalist and pro-imperialist regime of the Shah can only be welcomed. We are all in favor of a union with democratic forces, including the religious ones."[50]

This statement notwithstanding, the party felt isolated and in mid-January reorganized its leadership, replacing

Eskandari with Dr. Noureddin Kianouri. The latter promptly announced his party's support for Khomeini's Islamic Revolutionary Council, stating that the party program is quite compatible with the Ayatollah's action program.[51]

While the exiled leadership of the party was reorganizing and pondering moves to catch up with the revolutionary momentum in Iran, a number of recently released former Tudeh members organized a new political group known as the Democratic Union of Iranian People. In the final stage of revolution this group, led by A. Behazin, organized an impressive rally of nearly 10,000 people in Tehran who chanted such slogans as "Victory to the Tudeh Party," and "Neither Compromise nor Constitution but Armed Uprising."[52]

As we will see, the functions performed by numerous leftist groups in the revolutionary coalition were proportional to their organizational skill, the size of their following, and that sense of timing so essential in achieving political goals.

6

Stages of Revolutionary Process

The revolutionary assault on the Iranian regime underwent several stages, each characterized by distinct features both with respect to strategy and participants. In each stage the revolutionary process was accelerated as much by the action of the revolutionary coalition as by measures taken by the regime.

The first stage began on January 9, 1978, when Khomeini's supporters rioted in Qom, and ended with the collapse of the Amuzegar government August 27, 1978 and the premiership of the Sharif-Emami. The second stage corresponded with Sharif-Emami's tenure, in which martial law was declared and a number of serious clashes took place, resulting in heavy civilian casualties.

The third stage began on November 6, when the near-total collapse of order in the capital city prompted the Shah to install a military government led by General Gholamreza Azhari, the Chairman of the Joint Chiefs of the Iranian Armed Forces. This period was highlighted by massive disturbances in the holy month of Moharram (December 2-December 29), and ended with the installation of Bakhtiar's civilian government and the departure of the Shah on January 16.

The fourth and final stage corresponded with the period between January 16 and February 11. During this phase the revolutionary forces seized power by way of insurrectional moves which first neutralized and then caused the total disintegration of the armed forces.

First Stage: Protest Movement

The first stage of this process may be characterized as the least revolutionary, because the above-described coalition as yet neither advocated the overthrow of the monarchical regime nor resorted to illegal or extralegal methods in its opposition to the regime. At this stage the anti-regime coalition could be viewed as a protest movement opposing three basic conditions in Iran:

a) A repressive regime which was simply not capable of self-reform. Under more normal circumstances the protest should have led to demands for free elections, revision of the Constitution, and transformation of the absolute dynastic control to a constitutional monarchical one.

Indeed, some participants in this phase of the struggle voiced such demands. Among them were Shia leaders within the country and most notably Ayatollah Shariatmadari, the moderate group within the National Front (with the exclusion of Bazargan's Iran's Liberation Movement), non-Marxist factions in the intelligentsia and the bulk of the *bazaari*. Throughout the summer when the Majlis was permitted some measure of legitimate dissent, half a dozen deputies broke away from Rastakhiz and began to articulate the goals and grievances of the anti-regime coalition. Led by Bani-Ahmed the dputy from Tabriz, (the site of the first civilian uprising in

February), this group became increasingly vocal and ultimately joined the more extremist groups.

b) The protest was directed against the economic disparity and social injustices which had played a significant role in alienating the politically significant strata of the population. Few participants in the movement agreed upon the methods of generating a more egalitarian society. For Moslem fundamentalists that society meant a return to a purely Islamic system of taxation and social services. For the non-Marxist left it meant a type of Iranian socialism. For the Marxist left it meant the total destruction of private property and the Western model of a mixed and capitalist economy.

Certainly at this stage of the struggle the leading groups of participants did not believe that the state apparatus should be seized in order to construct a new egalitarian economic system. The prevailing belief was that once the first objective of the movement was achieved, the second would follow naturally. A democratic and multi-party political system would be able to formulate policies and priorities conducive to the establishment of a more "just" socio-economic system in Iran.

c) The last target of this protest movement was the pronounced pro-Western posture of Iran's foreign policy. To many opponents of the government, Iran's pro-Western alignment was a clear manifestation of the authoritarian regime's economic philosophy and one which was designed to protect Western and notably American military-economic interests.

The secular groups led by the National Front were prominent advocates of the genuine non-alignment vigorously pursued by the late Dr. Mossadegh in the early 1950's. They believed that the Shah's "positive equilibrium" amounted to balancing concessions to one superpower by granting new ones to the other. Instead, these groups preferred the guiding concept of a "negative equilibrium." This stance would be negative in terms of superpower interests, since it would deny economic and military concession to them both, but positive with respect to Iran's national interest, since it would reject alignment with either.

Although the leftist groups supported non-alignment as a broad concept, they had other motives for rejecting the regime's foreign policy. To them Iran's client-state status meant nothing less than being a surrogate state for the United States. Among other drawbacks, this status made Iran the protector of a whole host of conservative and archaic states in the Persian Gulf. Finally, the more Islamic fundamentalist groups in the opposition had a grievance against Iran's policy vis-a-vis the Arab-Israeli zone of conflict. For them the sale of oil to Israel, its de facto recognition by Iran and the evidence of Israeli involvement in training Iran's security personnel were anti-Islamic and anti-national.

Both action and inaction by the regime during this stage bore heavily on the development and acceleration of the protest movement. The most notable action was the policy of liberalization. Although this had begun prior to President-elect Carter's inauguration in January 1977, it received a major impetus when the Policy of Human Rights was enunciated by the new Democratic administration.

What motivated the Shah to espouse the liberalization policy may be summarized as:

a) A desire to pave the way for the transition of power to his son when he came of age. The Shah was much impressed by the Spanish experience in which the transition from authoritarian regime to a pluralistic parliamentary system was relatively trouble-free, and he wished to accomplish the same for Iran. He believed what had been done in Spain after the dictator's death could be done in Iran while the absolutist monarch was still in power.

b) Undoubtedly the American advocacy of human rights also played a role. During both his last visit to the United States in November 1977 and the Carter visit in 1978, the Shah was urged to accelerate the process of liberalization. This policy included an end to the torture of political prisoners, their selective release, an attempt to introduce legal reforms, and a loosening of tight censorship.[53]

There is little dispute that the effect of the Carter advocacy of human rights was to raise the expectations of the opposition. However, there is considerable disagreement as to the relative weight that this policy brought to bear upon the regime. One important leader of the secular opposition referred to this phenomenon in a way which is clearly compatible with Crane Brinton's concept of revolutionary outbreak at the moment of rising expectations. Mehdi Bazargan has characterized the revolt as "the result of 25 years of cruelty, oppression, and corruption. We did not believe the Shah when he started the liberalization policy, but when Carter's human rights drive lifted the hope of the people, all the built-up pressure exploded."[54]

Associated with the liberalization policy was the Shah's pledge to conduct a free election for the Majlis session due in June 1979. As our study of the failure of the one-party system indicated, the regime had not accepted the logical consequences of a free election, that is, the emergence of centers of legitimate dissent in and out of the parliament.

Nonetheless, on the occasion of Constitution Day, August 5, the Shah unequivocally pledged complete freedom in the next elections and espoused a multi-party system. Evidence of the abruptness of this change of policy was inadvertently provided by his own prime minister, who a week earlier had categorically emphasized Iran's continuation as a one-party state.

The Shah's pledge was not taken seriously, however, for by

49

then his credibility had been badly eroded. Even the moderate members of the protest movement were inclined to dismiss his pledge as either a mask or a concession which had come too late and had done too little to satisfy their fundamental demands.

Some among them wondered what was the reason for waiting until 1979. Did not the Shah possess the option of dissolving the Majlis and calling for a new election? Could he not demand that the Rastakhiz deputies resign en masse, thus expediting a new election? In retrospect, his failure to have done so seems to have been critical. His inaction was undoubtedly based on a profound suspicion that a free election so soon would produce a parliament which would be an independent and competing source of legitimate power. Morever, with such a parliament there was the intolerable risk that the legitimacy of the monarchical regime itself might be questioned.

The "King Carlos" formula of peaceful transition to a constitutional monarchy was not accepted in its entirety, for the Shah was fully aware of the role that Dr. Mossadegh's eight-man parliamentary group of the National Front had played in the 16th Majlis, from 1949 to 1951. The influence of this group had been totally disproportionate to its numerical strength. In fact, this minority was so dominant that the Majlis adopted oil nationalization laws and indeed, in April 1951 and July 1952 had even imposed its leader as prime minister on the reluctant Shah.[55]

To summarize, the first stage ended with the resignation of Amuzegar, whose anti-inflation policies had aggravated the *bazaari* and whose handling of the Abadan cinema arson on August 24 had convinced the Shah of the necessity for more concrete concessions and the reversal of selected policies. The Shah's Constitution speech dramatically pulled the rug from under Amuzegar and his departure was then simply a matter of time.

Second Stage: Concessions and Martial Law

The appointment of Sharif-Emami marked the beginning of the period of concrete concessions designed to placate and defuse the opposition. However, instead of satisfying the opposition, these concessions were interpreted as signs of weakness and further emboldened it to escalate its demands. Moreover, the new prime minister's loyalty to the Shah and his long tenure of service to the crown convinced the more radical secular and religious groups of the opposition that the Shah continued to underestimate the intensity and depth of resentment against his absolutist dynastic control.

To appease the clergy, Sharif-Emami reinstated the Moslem solar calendar which had been replaced four years before by the so-called Imperial calendar. (In an attempt to start numbering the years from the coronation of Cyrus and the beginning of the Persian Empire, about 1100 years had been added.) The regime also abolished the cabinet position of women's affairs and pledged a review of all recent legislative acts to make them more compatible with Islamic tenets.

To mollify the secular opposition, the Shah formally disavowed the ruling single party, restored a large measure of freedom to the press amounting to nearly lifting censorship, and decreed that there would now be freedom of assembly and speech.[56]

Nonetheless, between the formation of his cabinet and September 7 when martial law was declared in twelve major cities, the country witnessed numerous riots, demonstrations, civil disobedience, and sporadic strikes in both the private and public sectors. One measure of the strength of the opposition was the participation of the religious groups on

Eide-Fetr at the end of Ramadan on September 4, 1978, and the massive public prayer and the impressive parades which preceded and followed it. Over a million participants demanded such non-revolutionary changes as the reinstatement of the 1906 Constitution, the release of political prisoners, and an end to corruption. In response, the new government attempted to regulate future mass rallies by submitting a bill on free speech and assembly to the Majlis, but the parliament never voted on it.

Emboldened by the success of the Eide-Fetr rally, the opposition forces continued to test the limits of government tolerance by staging numerous demonstrations, especially in provincial towns, one of which, Isfahan, had already been under martial law since August. On September 7 the cabinet approved the decree to impose martial law in twelve additional cities, including Tehran.

That declaration had not been fully publicized nor had government threats been taken seriously. As a result, the next morning the major clash which occurred in Tehran's Jaleh Square brought the military into open confrontation with the opposition forces. Several hundred unarmed civilians, including women and children, lost their lives and thus became the first victims of the new martial law administration.

The events of this "Black Friday" and the highly emotional and histrionic funeral ceramony for the victims at the main Tehran cemetary had a sobering effect on the more moderate groups within the opposition. The non-revolutionary clergy vehemently condemned the martial law administration.[57] To the radicals of the left and the right, that confrontation graphically confirmed their conviction that the new government was as subservient to the Shah as the previous one. The turn of events enhanced the guerrillas' success in recruitment, and for the first time the opposition took on the army, almost totally ignoring the civilian government.

The "Black Friday" massacre also played into the hands of the exiled Khomeini, who as early as July, had urged his followers to accumulate weapons and train themselves in their use.

Two tactics were used to neutralize and infiltrate the army. One aimed particularly at conscripts, appealing to their sense of fraternity with the civilian population and to their sense of religion by reminding the soldiers of the religious sanctions for opposition activities. Mullahs from provincial towns were carefully assigned to concentrations of troops from the same provincial backgrounds. These religious leaders could invoke the name and prestige of the provincial clergy and they often communicated to the troops in their provincial tongues or dialect the admonition not to fire on their fellow citizens.

The second tactic was the threat of retaliation against army officers and their families. In addition, there were efforts to implant the seeds of dissension between the higher ranking, often well-to-do officers and the junior, less affluent ones.

The civilian government exhibited considerable indecisiveness. Partly because the martial law had prevented it from the effective exercise of authority and partly because it still believed in working within the system, the government attempted to balance the repression of martial law with liberalizing reforms. A free press and live broadcasts of Majlis debates often involved serious attacks on the army and even some indirect criticism of the Shah by assailing corruption in his family.

The opposition perceived this duality of policy as a further sign of the weakness of royal authority. The opposition, which was gradually becoming more radicalized, decided that martial law should be defied and demanded its termination. Its request for the immediate release of all political prisoners would now be included in repeated declarations enacted throughout the country in the course of many "unauthorized" rallies.

As yet, however, the opposition as a whole did not demand an end to the monarchy, though serious efforts were undertaken by the Khomeini and Marxist groups to persuade both less combative Ayatollahs, notably Shariatmadari in Qom, and the National Front that the protest movement now should become a revolutionary one. These efforts stressed the view that half measures of a reformist nature were doomed and that the defiance of martial law itself was a revolutionary action which should be acknowledged as such. Furthermore, since martial law was the military arm of the monarch, its defiance meant a direct challenge to royal authority and its legitimacy.

Late in October two other developments of potentially devastating significance occurred. First, the academic year began, thereby providing a rallying point and organizational focus for opposition forces. Second, a wave of general strikes, deceptively non-political in nature, began to plague the country.

The civilian government entered into immediate negotiations with the striking workers and civil servants, often granting them huge wage increases which ranged from 30 to 100 percent. In an attitude reminiscent of the one displayed in the French crisis of May 1968, the regime believed that the workers who had prospered under various pro-labor legislation could be mollified.[58]

The most devastating of the strikes occurred in the oil industry in which Iran's nearly 6 million barrel a day production was reduced by 60 percent at the end of October. Having been offered substantial pay raises, the workers promptly returned to work, only to resume the strikes shortly thereafter. But now, significantly, the strikes assumed a political character. Under the guise of supporting an end to martial law, freedom of political prisoners, and the return of political exiles, the strikers were joining the more radical opposition groups and agitating for progressively more revolutionary demands.

At the end of this stage, Dr. Karim Sanjabi, the leader of the secular National Front, finally succumbed to the pressures from both its left and the Khomeini faction and declared that the Front, too, would work outside the system. He declared the monarchy illegal and asked for a general referendum to ascertain the preference of the people for a different political system.

In early November Dr. Sanjabi met with Khomeini in the Paris suburb of Neauphle-le-Chateau. There he joined the Ayatollah in two common objectives: the ouster of the Shah and the refusal to cooperate in any face-saving and non-violent means for the Shah's departure. A public referendum was still advocated but under the pressure of fast-moving events, whether it should sanction a *fait accompli* or should legitimize a change of regime before the fact became an academic question. It is clear, however, that acceptance of Khomeini's views by the National Front leadership marked the highpoint of revolutionary developments, for it brought the best known and most persistent forces of the intelligentsia into conformity with the radical opposition. In a sense by this time the vast majority of the regime's opponents were in agreement with the goals the extremist groups had espoused in the first stage of the revolution. The success of these gorups in recruiting the National Front legitimized the revolutionary struggle.

On November 3 and 4 the reopened univesity became the arena for the first open anti-Shah riot, thereby leading to the third stage of revolutionary development. As to the role of the Sharif-Emami government in this transition, it must be recalled that apart from the demoralizing impact of its indecisiveness on the army, the regime failed both to dissolve the parliament and to fix a firm date for a new election. Instead, it launched an anti-corruption campaign which discredited some former government officials but did little to establish its own credibility. The release of nearly half of some 3,000 political prisoners not only exposed the extent of repressiveness of the regime but reinforced the ranks of extremists, many of whose leaders had served time in prison. In the final stage of insurrection the two guerrilla movements which bore the brunt of the street fighting were led by some of these recently freed prisoners.

Furthermore, some accounts indicated that freed trade union officials of the Tudeh and its affiliated United Council returned to the major industrial centers and played a significant role in the formation and conduct of strikes.[59]

Third Stage: Revolutionary Radicalization

This stage began with the bloody riots on November 5 and the subsequent replacement of Sharif-Emami's cabinet by the military government of General Gholamreza Azhari. It ended with the resignation of Azhari and the departure of the Shah on January 16, following the parliament's acceptance of the civilian cabinet of Shahpur Bakhtiar.

The riots of November 5 were triggered by two days of clashes between security forces and dissident students at Tehran University. Bolstered by the radicalization of the National Front and supported by hundreds of university professors whose sit-in had been forcibly broken up by the security forces, students attempted to topple a statue of the Shah at the entrance of the university. As a result of several casualties from these clashes, the military units weere severely reprimanded and vehement protests were made in the still functioning Majlis.

The following morning officers in charge of security around the university withdrew and allowed the protestors a free hand. Joined by the *bazaari* and high school students and emboldened by a minimum of resistance, the protesters went on a destructive rampage looting and burning banks, hotels, and government buildings.

Armed guerrillas attacked several police stations and for the first time the slogan, "Death to the Shah" was shouted in defiance and in unison by the protesters.

In a panicky response to the turn of events the Shah addressed the people in a last-ditch effort to divert the course of the revolutionary struggle. In a desperate attempt to coopt the revolutionary forces he declared: ". . .In the open political atmosphere gradually developed in these two recent years you, the Iranian nation, have risen against cruelty and corruption. This revolution cannot but be supported by me the King of Iran." He then admitted his failure to persuade his opponents to form a coalition government, pledging that nonetheless, his new and temporary government would eliminate corruption and repression and restore social justice after the ". . .sacrifices you have made."[60]

The Shah's moves at this stage seem to have been motivated by several considerations:

First, the military cabinet was not led by such hardliners as General Oveisi, the Military Governor of Tehran and the commander of the army, but by a moderate general known for his dislike of politics and commonly regarded as a softliner. The choice of General Azhari was due to the Shah's fear that the appointment of a tough military leader would risk an erosion of his remaining authority. Knowing that the mourning month of Moharram, which was approaching, presented strong potential for disturbances and bloodshed, the Shah contemplated a familiar scenario. This was the prospect of a coup d'etat of the type his own father had staged in

February 1921 in the name of law and order but as a prelude to the ouster of Ahmed Shah, the discredited last ruler of the Qajar dynasty.

Second, the military government coexisted with and indeed was formally approved by the parliament. The Majlis had not been dissolved, even after confirming the new ministry, despite some cabinet members' understanding that this would occur. The Shah's refusal to dissolve the parliament stemmed from his belief that parliament could balance the authority of the military regime and effectively rule out an unauthorized military coup d'etat. In a crisis he could appeal to the Majlis against a disloyal army or to a loyal army against a threatening Majlis.

Third, a further move by the Shah was designed to undermine the unity of the revolutionary coalition. By seeking to recruit the leader of the National Front and releasing imprisoned clergy leaders such as Ayatollah Taleghani, he hoped to come up with leaders who could compete effectively with Khomeini.

None of these suppositions proved tenable. The consequence of the first and second measures was that both the Majlis and the military were paralyzed in their ability to deal with the now self-confident and quite cohesive revolutionary coalition. The army could not act decisively either by staging a royalist coup or by overthrowing the monarchy, and in time it joined the less radical forces of opposition. The Majlis, similarly, was neutralized, although it could have taken any number of measures. The enactment of a bill for a referendum on the legitimacy of the monarchical system, for instance, would have preempted one of the most important demands of the opposition. Or it might simply have voted into office an opposition leader either from the National Front or some of the moderate leaders of the Shia clergy.

In short, though dominated by the Shah's hand-picked

candidates of the single Rastakhiz party, the Majlis was unlikely to show compunction in taking any of the above anti-regime actions.

As to the last measure, namely a continuous attempt to cause discord within the ranks of the National Front and urge a new coalition cabinet, it had become evident that in light of the radicalization of the movement such an effort was already too late. Nonetheless, throughout this stage the Shah approached various National Front leaders, including Dr. Gholam Hosein Sadighi, Karim Sanjabi, and finally Shahpur Bakhtiar to find a replacement for the military cabinet. As we will see, when Bakhtiar finally agreed to form a cabinet, it was on the condition that the Shah depart and in a fashion that did not denote coalitional agreement among any significant oppposition groups.

It is clear that the idea of forming a coalition cabinet when various forces of opposition could only agree on the ouster of the regime was at best wishful thinking and at worst deceptive and even counterproductive. In pursuance of the elusive goal of installing a coalition cabinet the Shah was fully supported by the United States but virtually by no one in Iran. Henry Kissinger has written about the folly of pursuing this goal in order to mollify revolutionary forces. The fundamental challenge of a revolution, he notes, is for the government to forestall revolution by making timely concessions. Wise governments do not consider adaptation as concession but as part of a natural process of increasing popular support.

"But when a revolution is in train, it cannot then be moderated by concessions. Once it has occurred, the pre-eminent requirement is the restoration of authority."[61] In Iran the frantic concessions which the regime offered in the very midst of revolution and particularly in its third stage, could not rectify the situation.

Undoubtedly the Shah's search for a coalition government

was viewed as such a concession at the time when to quote Kissinger, "political factions were killing each other in the street precisely because they cannot agree on the minimum necessity for a political contest."

In reaction to the installation of General Azhari's government, the revolutionary coalition accelerated its demands. It refused to accept the legitimacy of any element of the Iranian system. Not only must the Shah go, but also the military government appointed by him must be dissolved. The Majlis was equally illegal. With the approach of Moharram the religious frenzy was building for the final assault on the regime.

Government behavior during Moharram was confused and uncertain. Even though in the past, religious processions have been sanctioned under all conditions, the government banned all demonstrations during the month. The military authorities, however, could not enforce a curfew and ban on public meetings in the face of massive outcries of defiance. Rooftops, neighborhoods, and local mosques became assembly points for thousands of people whose chants of Allaho-Akbar (God is great) echoed in the night.

General strikes by power workers left the fate of the city in the hands of opponents who could simply black out selected sections of the town in order to paralyze the security forces or deny access of the state radio and television to the citizenry.

On the third day of Moharram the government lifted the ban on religious processions for Tassua and Ashura, the 9th and 10th of December. In another conciliatory measure it released the National Front leader Karim Sanjabi, who, even while in jail had been taken for an audience with the Shah in order to persuade him to form a coalition government.

On December 10, the ninth day of Moharram, a massive parade and rally was held in Tehran. Over a million people responded to the joint call of the religious and political

60

leaders and demanded dissolution of the military government, removal of the illegal Shah, and their replacement by an Islamic Republic. This demonstration was predominantly religious in tone and in organization but an even larger rally and march on the following day, the Ashura, had more pronounced political objectives. Freedom of all political prisoners, severance of ties with Israel and South Africa, and full freedom for all political parties were now added to the previous demands.

Strenuous efforts were made to maintain order and discipline so that the regime's frequent charges of hooliganism and terrorism would be seen to be false. Though the security forces remained out of sight during both marches, attempts were made to recruit the army and the conscripts in particular. Appeals to a sense of fraternity with the soldiers were combined with a call for "a renewal of Islamic solidarity against forces of evil and oppression on this most holy day of Shia martyrdom."[62]

Attesting to the solid basis of support the revolutionary forces had mustered were the nearly five million participants in Ashura's demonstration in Tehran and provincial towns. In the wake of these huge demonstrations the Shah finally became convinced of the depth and intensity of popular feeling against his regime and renewed his search for an acceptable civilian government. With the outright refusal of Dr. Sanjabi and the failure of Dr. Sadighi, the National Front elder statesman, to cooperate, the Shah turned to Dr. Shahpur Bakhtiar. He agreed to form a cabinet in return for a number of crucial additional concessions from the Shah.

1) He insisted on the reinstatement of the practice of ascertaining the support of the Majlis before a prime minister is named. This practice, abandoned by the Shah after the ouster of Dr. Mossadegh in 1953, was viewed as the essence of parliamentary democracy, for it virtually made the Shah's

designation of the head of government subject to Majlis veto.

This agreement was a major concession to Bakhtiar, but the revolutionary coalition, which included Bakhtiar's own National Front, interpreted it as a compromising action. The coaltion criticized the practice as reinforcing the legitimacy of the parliament and indirectly that of the Shah himself. As noted earlier, the revolutionary coalition had rejected every vestige of the state apparatus as illegal; hence it regarded Bakhtiar's utilization of a disused parliamentary practice as anathema to its objective. In its view, acceptance of the charge of forming a civilian government was tantamount to acceptance of a constitutional monarch, or the so-called "King Carlos" formula, as a viable option.

2) Another sine qua non for Bakhtiar was assurance that the military would accept his government. He required changes in the command structure and the appointment to his government of several retired army generals who had impeccable reputations for honesty and even some evidence of opposition to the Shah's repressive regime. The Shah saw Bakhtiar as the last chance and therefore made every effort to obtain the military's pledge of allegiance to the new civilian government. He did so, even though it required the dismissal or transfer of such hardliners as General Oveisi, the commander of the army and General Manuchehr Khosradad, the commander of the paratroopers.

3) By far the most important pledge to Bakhtiar was the Shah's agreement to leave the country "on vacation" just as soon as both houses of parliament gave his government the final vote of approval. This pledge effectively foreclosed any chance of a royalist coup by the army, for it felt a sense of abandonment, aggravated by signs of disintegration within its own ranks.

As far as the opposition groups were concerned, the significance of the Shah's departure seemed lost to them.

Mindful of the 1953 coup during the Shah's temporary absence, some opposition leaders bitterly attacked Bakhtiar for collaborating with the Shah. His former colleagues in the leadership of the National Front which had expelled him feared that he would be able to split the opposition. On December 25 the combined forces of opposition once more rejected any form of cooperation with the civilian government as long as the Shah remained in power.

The third stage ended with the Shah's departure on January 16. This phase was characterized by the intensification of revolutionary mobilization and the virtual neutralization of Iran's armed forces. It was also marked by a gradual acceptance of the inevitability of the overthrow of the dynasty. The opposition was now more than ever determined to work outside the constitutional framework. It was convinced that the massive rallies in the first 10 days of Moharram constituted a "public referendum" against the Shah's monarchy and for Khomeini's Islamic Republic. Just as Lenin interpreted the collapse of Russian resistance in the spring of 1917 as Russian soldiers voting for his cause by their fleeing feet, the Iranians also seemed to be saying that "our people, too, voted for the revolution and its political goals by their feet."

Final Stage: Insurrectional Assault

Between January 16 and February 11 Iran was in a state of total chaos. In the vacuum created by the Shah's departure the three remaining political forces were the civilian remnants of the state apparatus, (the Majlis and the Regency Council), the Bakhtiar government, and the demoralized and confused army. Each of these elements was in a different state of disarray. Since their perceptions of political objectives were different and even contradictory, they could not present a united and cohesive force.

For a time it seemed they all supported the vague notion that all changes, even a transformation to a republic, must take place in the context of the 1906 Constitution. The prime minister even invoked the memory of Dr. Mossadegh, who had drastically reduced the Shah's power and even sent him into temporary exile — all within the confines of Iran's constitution.

The radical opposition, on the other hand, argued that the National Front failed precisely because Dr. Mossadegh sought to act within those confines. To work within these limits was anti-revolutionary; it would simply contribute to the incompletion of the revolutionary process, just as the original constitutional movement in 1906-1911 and the Nationalist Movement in 1950-53 had done. More specifically, the immediate problem for both the opposition and the government was the return of Khomeini to Iran.

In view of Khoemeini's insistence that Bakhtiar's government was illegal and that he, too, must resign, the prime minister was placed in a critical dilemma. Permitting Khomeini to return would have meant a confrontation with him, his shadow cabinet, and the Islamic Revolutionary Council which had been constituted secretly from among the pro-Khomeini clergy in Iran. To oppose his return would have meant risking continuous civil disorder and an almost exclusive reliance on the dispirited army to maintain the government in power.

The sense of isolation of the civilian government was reinforced in another mass march on January 19. At this rally, which coincided with "Arbain," the fortieth day after Imam Hossein's death, a 10-point resolution was read. This declaration urged the abolition of the Pahlavi dynasty and appealed to the armed forces, the still functioning Majlis, and the recently formed Regency Council to join the movement.[63]

This massive display of unified determination was followed

by several tactical measures designed by the revolutionary coalition to further intensify the government's dilemma.

a) It declared the Shah-appointed government a fraudulent gesture calculated to pave the way for a pro-Shah military coup.

b) It urged the continuation of massive strikes in all sectors of public life until the government resigned.

c) It began intensive recruitment within the army, by dwelling on the futility of further bloodshed in support of an exiled and discredited Shah.

d) Most significantly, it began to set up parallel revolutionary committees in provincial towns and in the bazaar area of Tehran. These committees gradually took over all governmment functions, including food distribution, a measure reminiscent of the separatist takeover in Azarbayjan in November-December 1945. In this situation also the gradual erosion of the authority of the government had left its last remnant, namely the military, isolated and susceptible to imminent collapse.[63]

In the last three weeks of this stage the authority of the Bakhtiar government was confined to the wealthier sections of Tehran. With such limited authority the government appeared to be increasingly restricted in its options regarding the most pressing issue of Khomeini's return. First the government closed the country's airports. Then Bakhtiar offered to travel to Paris and meet Khoemeini — an offer which was refused unless the prime minister resigned.

Finally, on February 1 Khomeini returned triumphantly to Tehran. The massive welcome rally served to underscore several salient matters. It convinced Khomeini of the wisdom of his uncompromising stand. It showed the army that public support for the revolutionary cause had not abated. And it convinced both the Majlis and the Regency Council tht the Bakhtiar cause was lost.

A constitutional solution to the crisis under which the Majlis would be presented a new cabinet with a number of Khomeini's appointees was summarily rejected by the revolutionaries. Instead, on February 6 the Ayatollah named Mehdi Bazargan as prime minister and urged the dual revolutionary organizations, namely the strike committees and the Islamic revolutionary committees, to intensify their efforts toward bringing down the government.

At about the same time erosion in the army's support for Bakhtiar became more evident. In daily marches and rallies groups of army units mingled with civilians. The high command, led by General Abbas Gharabaghi, the Chairman of the Joint Chiefs, was secretly negotiating with Bazargan and Khomeini to pave the way for the peaceful switch of the army's allegiance to the provisional revolutionary government. However, the disunity within the high command prevented this from happening. It was left to a military clash among army units to trigger the collapse of the army and hence the Bakhtiar government during February 9-11.

On February 8 a last massive march was held in support of Khomeini and his designated prime minister. Next day units of Royal Guards known as Javidan (The Immortals) tried to end the sit-down strike by several hundred air force conscripts. Some sixty deaths among the latter were the result.

Late in the evening of February 10 units of Javidans attacked air force technicians (Homafaran), and cadets in Farahabad and Doshantappeh bases, trying to subdue their strikes and demonstrations in favor of Khomeini.[65] However, the Javidans were unable to subdue them, partly because these bases were located in the lower class section of eastern Tehran and partly because news of the attack brought in armed guerrillas of Mojahedin and Fedayin to support the air force insurrectionists.

66

Instead, the insurrectionists within these bases attacked the armory and began distributing weapons and ammunition to the civilians who had rushed to their defense. At one point a wall of revolutionaries placed themselves between reinforcements supporting the Royal Guards and insurrectionists within the base. In desperation the army declared a noon to 4 p.m. curfew, which was promptly denounced by Khomeini. He warned the army that failure to surrender would result in his declaration of "Jehad" or holy war. The holy war is a religious war against the infidel and its threat influenced many conscripts, and caused them to desert their bases. Others handed over their weapons to the swelling ranks of guerrillas which now included turbanned mullahs.

The climax of insurrection came on Sunday, February 11. In the early morning hours bands of guerrillas attacked twelve police stations in Tehran, setting many of them afire after confiscating weapons and distributing them to civilian insurrectionists. By noon the radio station had been taken over and used to relay instructions to fellow insurrectionists involved in street fighting. Units of air force cadets and other conscripts increasingly joined in to demobilize the two important military bases in Jamshidiyeh and Jay near the Tehran International airport. Having failed to subdue the rebellious troops, the Royal Guards retreated to their base at Lavizan which is within a mile from the Shah's Niavaran palace in northern Tehran.

By late afternoon the Supreme Council of the Armed Forces declared its "neutrality" in the struggle between Khomeini and Bakhtiar. Bakhtiar then submitted his resignation and fled into exile. By late evening every military installation except the military base of the Royal Guard and the Shah's palace were in the hands of the insurrectionists, as were all twenty-three police stations in Tehran. Through radio broadcasts the revolutionary government

67

communicated the collapse of the government to provincial centers.

By Monday morning the remaining centers were also taken over and Bazargan installed himself in the prime minister's headquarters. The residence of the Ayatollah in another section of downtown served as the provisional headquarters for the revolutionaries. It was here that scores of civilian and military leaders, some captured when the central Gasr prison was attacked and some who had surrendered during the chaos of the preceding two days, were assembled. Here also the Islamic Revolutionary Council established its provisional headquarters and tried to coordinate the activities of scores of *ad hoc* revolutionary committees with those of the strike committees throughout the country.

The revolutionary transition of power was thus completed after nearly thirteen months of violent struggle.

The Army's Disintegration

An analysis of the triumph of revolutionary forces must consider above all the performance of the army. As observed earlier, the army could not act decisively in the various stages of the revolution. Among the reasons which may explain its performance, the following stand out:

First, the prolonged "war of attrition" gradually had demoralized the army. Although martial law had been declared in the second stage of the revolution, the army was not given carte blanche to quell civil disturbances. Both during Sharif-Emami's term of office and later when the military government of General Azhari took over, the army felt it could not effectively enforce martial law. Particularly during Sharif-Emami's tenure when the Majlis debates were broadcast live and the press enjoyed a large measure of freedom, the army had been subjected to considerable restraint.

Second, the departure of the Shah denied the army the focus of loyalty and attention which only the Shah was able to project. In retrospect, the opponents of the regime had neutralized the army by paving the way for the Shah's departure. The prospect of a repeat performance of August 1953 when a temporarily exiled Shah could be brought back within a few days by a combined CIA-military operation seemed rather remote even to those who had not lost faith in the army's devotion to the throne.

Third, structural changes within the army since 1963 when it had brutally suppressed the religious uprising had made for a lack of solidarity. Under the Shah's aegis a rigid division between the three services had been imposed, making it impossible for commanders to communicate with each other except through him. The Chief of Staff had become a glorified quartermaster general, dealing with budgetary and logistical problems. The open break between the army and the air force and the relatively early participation of the latter in the revolution was partially due to this situation.

The Shah's command structure kept separate each corps — the infantry, artillery, armored vehicles, etc. In the armies of most countries, according to one observer, officers who reach the rank of brigadier can take command of units of other corps. Thus the more senior officers are a cohesive body of men bound together by their inter-corps experience. That kind of situation was anathema to the Shah, who feared it was conducive to a conspiratorial spirit. He decreed that no senior officer of one corps should ever command units of another corps.[66]

Fourth, the Shah believed in prestige and safety in numbers, fearing that it was easier to plot a coup with a small compact army or air force. Therefore, he expanded the army from 192,000 men in 1972 to 300,000 in 1976. But in order to expand the army, more officers had to be recruited from the

69

middle classes. As a result, a higher proportion of the troops were conscripts. The social background of such officers and men made them vulnerable to anti-Shah sentiment, particularly under such strong and sustained pressure as existed in the last six months of 1978.

Fifth, vast military expenditures proved to be counter-productive, for they meant fewer resources for economic development and consequently, more widespread discontent. Additionally, there was growing resentment against the thousands of foreign military experts.

Another cause of resentment was the Imperial Guards and the Rangers, which were entrusted with the task of protecting the royal family. The favored treatment given them antagonized other services whose support or at least acquiescence was needed for their effective functioning. And no doubt the counsel of American advisors against staging a coup in December and January played a role in demoralizing the armed forces.[67]

In the final analysis, however, the massive support for the opponents of the regime rendered the armed forces impotent to stage a military takeover. In the face of massive civil disobedience, martial law regulations could not be enforced. Moreover, despite its size and training, the army could not be used to break widespread strikes in the oil industry, transportation systems, and even the state airline. When the army was able to force oil workers back to the industry, it soon discovered that the physical presence of the workers was one thing and the actual resumption of their work quite another.

The distrust of air force pilots, similarly, prevented the utilization of their service to terminate the Iran Air strike. Doubts about the army's loyalty were in part due to the fact that the social composition of the lower ranking officers and conscripts did not radically differ from the civilian segments of the population. Even higher ranking officers were not confident that an attempted coup d'etat in the Shah's favor might not deviate from its indended goal.

Could a coup d'etat be undertaken to reinstate an indecisive and now departed Shah? Would it not be wiser to throw in the army's lot with the non-left religious opponents of the Shah? What were the chances that a secret leftist military conspiracy would not stage a coup within the coup if the army sought to reinstate a discredited Shah? After all, had not the communists been capable of infiltrating the army in the early 1950's when a similar upheaval against the regime had contributed to the military's demoralization?[68]

7

Conclusion

The bulk of this account has focused on the socio-political conditions in Iran immediately preceding the revolution, the function of the Shia hierarchy, the *bazaari,* and the intelligentsia in creating a broad coalition of revolutionary forces, and finally the various stages in the seizure of power and some of the immediate reasons for its success.

We saw how the protest movement became radicalized once dissident groups became convinced that the regime's self-correcting mechanism was slow and ineffective, and that the seizure of state power was imperative to the fulfillment of the aims of the protest movement.

This radicalization also manifested itself in rejecting the legitimacy of the state. Instead, the huge marches and rallies which characterized the third stage of the revolutionary process were presented as the foundation of a new legitimacy. These demonstrations were regarded as a referendum, more massive and more conclusive than any formal casting of ballots in opposition to the established political order.

With the radicalization of goals and strategies came the convergence of all revolutionary forces. There were at least three fundamental reasons for this coalescence. First, the groups had learned that none could achieve its goal in isolation. The religious uprising of June 1963, the student agitation over the last two decades, the urban guerrilla warfare since 1966, and the sporadic strikes by workers and government employees had all failed. Second, all opposition forces regarded the regime as being responsible for their alienation. Third, each saw that determined acts of civil disobedience could wrest concessions from the regime. The old solar Islamic calendar had been returned to the clergy along with a promise to make secular law more compatible with Islamic law. The intelligentsia secured the release of political prisoners and a large measure of freedom of the press. The *bazaari* saw an end to the government-sponsored anti-profiteering campaign.

In these concluding pages a preliminary characterization of the Iranian revolutionary upheaval will be presented.

Our first contention is that by any standard the Iranian upheaval must be considered a political revolution, which most simply is defined as "a sudden and violent overthrow of an established political order."[69] When reviewed as a more complex phenomenon, i.e., "sudden change in the social location of political power, expressing itself in the radical transformation of the process of government, of the official foundations of sovereignty or legitimacy," the Iranian experience would be even more qualified.[70]

As we reviewed the process of the transformation of the protest movement into a revolutionary one, we saw graphic evidence that this process entailed the total rejection of the legitimacy of the Pahlavi dynasty and a radical change in the location of power from the throne to the broad coalition of revolutionary forces presently embodied in Khomeini's

Islamic Revolutionary Council and the provisional government of Mehdi Bazargan.

But what characterizes the Iranian Revolution? Do the terms Islamic fundamentalist, or anti-Western do justice to this experience? Did the revolution mean different things to the various social groups which joined forces once they became convinced that the Iranian regime was incapable of reform?

We believe that the Islamic component of the Iranian revolution performed several crucial functions. First, it gave the movement the broadest possible popular base. Second, it put at the disposal of revolutionary forces the only available network of communication and mobilization, which was through the mosques and other religious centers. Third, at the critical third and fourth stages its armed guerrilla organization of Mojahedin played a significant role in the insurrectionary assault on the state apparatus. Fourth, the Shia clergy was instrumental in swaying elements of the armed forces away from the government by utilizing the symbolic concepts of "Jehad" and Fraternity with the Moslem civilian population.

Having acknowledged this, we than contend that the clergy by itself is unlikely to have been capable of unleashing the forces of revolution, as judged by the fifteen-year period of fairly stable monarchical control since the June 1963 religious uprising.

Here the role of the intelligentsia as a most distinctive partner in the revolutionary coalition assumes paramount significance. For this social group "liberation" either as a release from oppression or as personal freedom was the most compelling dimension of the revolution. Hanna Arendt's conception of revolution as requiring both newness and violence was applicable to the Iranian case. She has written, "Only when change occurs in the sense of a new beginning, when violence is used to constitute an altogether different form of government, to bring about the formation of a new body politic, where the liberation from oppression aims at least at the constitution of freedom, can we speak of revolution."[71]

As for the resort to violence, it seems that in the process of transofrmation from protest to revolutionary movement both religious groups and the intelligentsia did so, to quote Chalmers Johnson, "in order to cause the system to change when all else had failed, and the very idea of revolution is contingent upon this perception of societal failure."[72]

A further observation has to do with the breakdown in the legitimate means of effecting political change. We contend that in terms of cumulative causes, this failure of the Iranian regime was particularly significant. Repeated efforts at coopting the intelligentsia and the institutionalization of legitimate dissent through two-party or one-party organization collapsed precisely because the Shah's perception of dissent was narrowly exclusive. Even when liberalization policies were launched, the regime made it clear that criticism of the monarchy and the armed forces was not an acceptable form of dissent.

With regard to some of the immediate causes of the Iranian revolutionary upheaval, we saw how the bazaar's middle-class merchants reacted to the credit crunch of 1976 as an abrupt interruption in the fulfillment of their heightened expectations. As far as this stratum of the alienated populace is concerned, its revolutionary transformation fits neatly into James Davies' J curve formulation. "When a long period of rising expectations and gratifications is followed by a short period during which expectations continue to rise while gratifications fall off sharply, the probability of civil violence against the government rises rapidly"[73]

A final conclusion is that the peaceful transformation of an absolutist regime to one which is less authoritarian is improbable and even impossible. As noted earlier, the Shah's desire to emulate the post-Franco Spanish evolution toward a pluralistic democracy was frustrated above all because he believed that he himself could preside over that transformation. Certainly other reasons such as the acute economic disparity, large-scale corruption, and the opposition of the institutionalized Shia clergy contributed to the rejection of the "King Carlos" formula by the politically articulate Iranians.

The Iranian revolution is still in process. Whether it will continue to be incomplete or experience countermoves from within its own ranks or from domestic forces outside these ranks remains to be seen. Twice in Iran's modern history revolutionary upheavals have deviated from their original course by a combination of external and internal forces. The Constitutional Revolution of 1906-1911 led to the chaos and anarchy that heralded Reza Khan's coup d'etat in 1921.

The nationalist movement of the early 1950's, which was political in substance and economic in form, led to the 1953 coup d'etat which reinstated Reza Khan's son and marked the beginning of a quarter of a century of the Second Pahlavi dictatorship. The religiously inspired riots of 1963 could be safely quelled because they were not backed by a broad coalition of revolutionary forces, as in 1978-79. In view of these experiences perhaps the safest prognosis is that this third Iranian revolution will also change in emphasis if not in objective.

NOTES

1. *Besouye Tamaddone Bozorg* (Toward the Great Civilization) is the title of the Shah's last work, published in the spring of 1978.

2. The two parties were named Melliyoun (Nationalists) and Mardom (People) with the latter designated as the loyal opposition. Leonard Binder, *Iran; Political Development in a Changing Society.* (Berkeley and Los Angeles: University of California Press, 1962) pp. 222 ff.

3. For a discussion of cooptation in Iran see James A. Bill, *The Politics of Iran: Groups, Classes and Modernization,* (Columbus: Charles E. Merrill, 1972).

4. Marvin G. Weinbaum, "Iran Finds a Party System: The Institutionalization of Iran Novin," *Middle East Journal,* 27 (Autumn 1973) pp. 228-239.

5. Text of address in *Kayhan International,* Tehran, March 14, 1975.

6. See *Assasnamehe Movaghate Hezbe Rastakhiz Mellate Iran* (Provisional Constitution of Iranian People Resurgence Party), (Tehran: Kayhan Publishing House, 1976).

7. Personal interview with a member of the Political Bureau of the party in July, 1977. Also "Bahse Azad" (Free Debate) *Rastakhiz* Newspaper, July 25-26, 1977.

8. Personal interview with Daryush Hoomayon, deputy secretary general of the party and former Minister of Information and Tourism, January 27, 1978, Tehran.

9. Text of address in *Kayhan International,* August 5, 1978.

10. Sepehr Zabih, *The Communist Movement in Iran* (Berkeley and Los Angeles: University of California Press, 1966) pp. 111-112, and Gholamhossein Razi, "Genesis of Party in Iran: A Case Study of the Interaction Between the Political System and Political Parties," *Iranian Studies,* 3 (Spring 1970), pp. 58-90.

11. For a discussion of the Nationalist Movement and the role of the National Front see Richrd W. Cottom, *Nationalism in Iran,* (Pittsburgh: University of Pittsburgh Press, 1964). Also, S. Zabih, *op. cit.,* pp. 166-207.

12. Marvin Zonis, "He Took All the Credit, Now He Gets All the Blame," *New York Times,* January 14, 1979.

13. Quoted in Joseph Kraft, "Letter from Iran," *The New Yorker,* December 18, 1978, p. 144.

14. *Ibid.*

15. *Ibid.,* p. 147.

16. James A. Bill, "Iran and the Crisis of '78," *Foreign Affairs,* Winter 78-79, p. 324.

17. For a perceptive analysis of some aspects of this issue see Joseph Eliash, "Misconceptions Regarding the Judicial Status of the Iranian 'Ulama,' " *International Journal of Middle East Studies,* vol. 10, No. 1, February 1979, pp. 9-25.

18. James A. Bill, *op. cit.,* p. 335.

19. Ayattolah Borujerdi was one who denounced the mild Land Reform Law of May 16, 1960 as unconstitutional. See Joseph Eliash, *op. cit.,* p. 9.

20. Quoted in Nicholas Gage, "Iran: Making of a Revolution," *New York Times Magazine,* December 17, 1978, p. 132.

21. The Family Protection Law adopted in 1976 went a long way toward granting women protection, including initiation of divorce procedures and restriction on polygamy. Text of law in *Ettelaat,* February 11, 1976.

22. Michael Fisher, "The Qum Report," quoted in *The New Yorker, op. cit.,* p. 135.

23. *Ibid.,* p. 137.

24. *Ibid.*

25. *Ibid.,* p. 136.

26. *Ibid.,* p. 138.

27. General Moghaddam, the last head of the Iranian State Security and Intelligence Organization, the SAVAK, quoted in Joseph Kraft, *op. cit.*

28. Ehsan Omeed, "Political Upheaval in Iran: The Radical Shiites Who Demonstrate Reject the Legitimacy of Monarchy," *Inquiry,* Nov. 13, 1978.

29. Abdul Reza Hejazi, *ibid.,* p. 17.

30. This is the 10th day of Moharram, a day of mourning for the death of Imam Hossein throughout the Moslem Shia communities.

31. Amir Taheri, "The Bazaar," *Kayhan International,* October 2, 1978.

32. *Ibid.*

33. On the practice of religious exploitation for political ends see papers by Nikki Keddie, Hamid Algar, and Gustav Thaiss, in *Scholars, Saints, and Sufis: Moslem Religious Institutions in the Middle East Since 1500,* ed. Nikki Keddie (Berkeley and Los Angeles: University of California Press, 1972).

34. For an impartial account of these see *Kayhan International,* October 2-4, 1978.

35. *New York Times Magazine,* December 17, 1978, p. 134.

36. Many leftist students reportedly had joined the government volunteers in order to incite opposition to it. *Kayhan International,* October 3, 1978.

37. Amir Taheri, *op. cit.*

38. Julien Bharier's *Economic Development of Iran, 1900-1970.* (New York: Oxford University Press, 1971) and Jahangir Amuzegar's *Iran: Economic Development Under Dualistic Conditions,* (Co-authored with M. Ali Fekrat, (Chicago: University of Chicago Press, 1971) are only two examples of a large volume of literature on this matter.

39. Personal interview with the late Dr. Hassan Arsanjani, July 7, 1972, Tehran.

40. Iran, Plan and Budget Organization, *Income Share in Urban and Rural Iran,* Tehran, 1975.

41. H. R. Alker, Jr. and B. M. Rusett, "Indices for Comparing Inequality," in R. L. Merrit and S. Rokkan, *Comparing Nations* (New Haven: Yale University Press, 1966) pp. 349-372.

42. This study was conducted by Irma Adelman for the *Netherlands Institute for Advanced Studies in Humanities and Social Science,* and is cited in Leonard Silk, "West's Concern Over Iran," *New York Times,* January 7, 1979.

43. Binder, *op. cit.,* pp. 286-287.

44. Zabih, *Communist Movement in Iran,* pp. 246-259.

45. "Hezbe Sosyaliste Kargarane Iran," Statement of Purpose and Party Program. *Kayhan,* Air Edition, January 24, 1979.

46. Based on information given by families of the victims. Compiled by the Iranian newspapers between January 17 and February 7, 1979.

47. Based on statistics in the Iranian newspapers, particularly *Kayhan* and *Ettelaat,* January 24-February 7, 1979.

48. ODPG's statement, "Revolution is not the monopoly of any one group." Quoted in *Kayhan,* Air Edition, January 24, 1979.

49. *The Economist,* London, February 3-9, 1979.

50. Cited in *The New Yorker,* December 18, 1978, p. 150.

51. See Statement of the Executive Board of the Central Committee of the Tudeh Party, quoted in *Kayhan,* Air Edition, January 31, 1979. Indicative of the party's disarray is the attack of Dr. Freydoun Keshavarz, one of its former exiled leaders, on the new secretary general as a Stalinist and his criticism of the Soviet Union for persistent support of the Shah. *Ibid.*

52. *Ibid.*

53. James A. Bill, "Iran and the Crisis of '78," pp. 323-342.

54. *New York Times Magazine,* December 17, 1978, p. 145.

55. Cottom, *Nationalism in Iran,* op. cit.

56. *Kayhan International,* August 25-28, 1978.

57. Ayatollah Mohammed Kazem Shariatmadari issued a vehement denunciation of the Martial Law Administration from Qom but at this juncture did not come out for the Shah's ouster. *Etelaat,* September 9, 1978.

58. Henry Kissinger has pointed out the difference between the France of 1968 and Iran of 1978. He asserts that European evolution from feudal to modern states was very long and crisis-prone, whereas Iran under the Shah tried to accelerate this process without undertaking the political construction which should have accompanied the economic. *The Economist,* London, February 10, 1979, p. 31-35.

59. Some French sources which had traditional contacts with the Tudeh leadership reported that up to 80 percent of the membership in Strike Coordinating Committees in various oil industry centers such as Abadan, Aghajari, and Masjed — Soleyman were affiliated with Marxist groups including the Tudeh party itself. *L'Express,* January 20, 1979.

60. Texts in *Kayhan International,* November 4, 1978.

61. *The Economist,* London, February 10, 1979, p. 34.

62. Communique issued by Committee of Religious Personalities in charge of Ashura public march, December 10, 1978.

63. Text in *Kayhan,* Air edition, January 24, 1979.

64. See S. Zabih, "Insurrection in Azarbayjan," in *The Communist Movement in Iran,* pp. 98-106.

65. Air Force cadets and technicians had been involved in a series of disobedient acts since at least December 1. At the major Shahrokhi air base near Hamedan in western Iran 2,800 of them staged a hunger strike in support of the opposition. Similar strikes took place in Isfahan, Ahwaz, and the Fighter Command base near Tehran Mehrabad airport. *Kayhan,* Air edition, January 24, 1979.

66. *The Economist,* London. *op. cit.*

67. Reference is to General Robert Huyser, the Deputy Commander of NATO, whose visit to Iran was commonly reported to have the dual purpose of dissuading the Iranian generals from staging a coup and insuring the safety of some of the sophisticated US arms delivered to Iran under the Shah's massive military buildup program. *Kayhan International,* January 18, 1979.

68. Zabih, *The Communist Movement in Iran,* pp. 209-210.

69. Carl J. Fridrich, "An Introductory Note on Revolution," in Fridrich, ed. *Revolution* (New York: Atherton, 1967), p. 5.

70. Eugene Kamenka, "The Concept of a Political Revolution," in Fridrich, ed. *Revolution,* p. 124.

71. Hannah Arendt, *On Revolution,* (New York: Viking, 1963), pp. 2, 21, et passim. The term liberation or freedom has been frequently used by Iranian political

parties and movements. It is significant to note that even Mehdi Bazargan's party, with close ties to the Shia clergy, was named "Iran's Liberation Movement."

72.   Chalmers Johnson, *Revolutionary Change,* (Boston: Little, Brown and Company, 1966), p. 12.

73.   James C. Davies, "The J-Curve Theory," *American Political Science Review,* (vol. 72, No. 4, December 1978), pp. 1357-58.

Postscript

Since the completion of this manuscript the Iranian revolutionary forces have proceeded to consolidate their power and to find a sense of direction with regard to a future political system. In pursuance of these objectives the revolutionary regime has faced many problems, the most troublesome of which has proven to be the task of institutionalizing the revolution or shifting from destructive to constructive policies and practices.

This postscript analyzes various dimensions of these problems, covering such events as the March 30-31 referendum, the problem of law and order and the gradual erosion of the solidarity of the revolutionary coalition.

Consolidation of Power

Once power was seized, the revolutionary coalition set out to consolidate its authority by a series of measures. First, a provisional cabinet was installed under the leadership of Mehdi Bazargan, with representation predominantly from his Iran's Liberation Movement and independent supporters of Khomeini, but also including the secular National Front. Neither of the two dominant guerrilla organizaitons, the Fedayin or the Mojahedin was given representation in the cabinet and soon they began to criticize the provisional government's failure to reward them.

Second, a small secret Revolutionary Council, headed by Khomeini, began to exercise both judicial and legislative powers. It presided over a vast number of revolutionary committees (Komiteh) throughout the country as well as Islamic Revolutionary tribunals set up to prosecute the chief collaborators of the old regime.

Third, from among strike coordinating committees in industry, business, ministries, universities and other organizatiuus there emerged a network of local committees, in theory accountable to regional revolutionary committees but in practice totally decentralized and virtually autonomous. The provisional government set out to operate in a traditional sense, based on the functional division of labor and collective responsibility. Almost immediately it was plagued by the nature of its relationship with the Revolutionary Council, its subordinate committees, Revolutionary tribunals, and to a lesser extent, with local committees.

In two areas the problems were particularly acute. One was the question of security and the other concerned the trials of the former regime's officials. The near total collapse of the military, the police, and the gendarmaries in the closing days of the revolution and the dispersal of large quantities of weapons among the insurrectionists made the task of restoring law and order extremely difficult. Khomeini's call for the return of an estimted 300,000 weapons to mosques and other collection points by and large went unheeded. Moreover, the provisional government could not rely on the support of either of the guerrilla groups to enforce the policy of weapons collection because both groups were excluded from the governmcnt. Indeed, to have relied on one would have further antagonized the other.

Apart from the two guerrilla organizations whose ranks had swelled in the final days of insurrection, a large number of younger civilians also were armed. These individuals formed a loose alliance of Moslem militia which obeyed the directives of the Revolutionary Council and the regional committees rather than the provisional government, even though the Council was represented in the government by Dr. Ibrahim Yazdi, deputy prime minister for revolutionary affairs.

The provisional government believed that the Iranian army could be reconstructed and in time could become the legitimate organ for the maintenance of law and order. The demoralization of the officer corps and the reluctance of the main guerrilla organizations to concur in the government decision made the reconstruction of the armed forces slow and extremely difficult. The Fedayin demanded the total abolition of the old army and the creation of a people's army modeled on the Chinese People's Liberation Army.

The Revolutionary Council seemed at least temporarily dependent on the Moslem Militia, renamed the Pasdarane Ingelab (Revolutionary guards). The Pasdaran exercised effective police power in Tehran and other major cities, and in March they were dispatched to help the regular army quell the uprisings of the Kurds in Sanandaj and the Turkamans in Gonbad Qabus. Both events convinced the Council that a reconstructed military was essential if the country was to avoid disintegration and even civil war. The government and the Council believed the Moslem Militia could be absorbed by the reorganized police in cities and the gendarmarie in rural areas.

Every attempt was made to mollify the remnants of the armed forces. In mid-April Khomeini declared a Revolutionary Islamic Armed Forces day in which military parades were organized. The Tehran police chief declared that in another two months all police stations would resume regular functions and at least 4000 Pasdarane with certificates of completion of elementary school would be assimilated into the reconstructed force.

Whether these measures will proceed expeditiously remains to be seen. Instances of lawlessness and political assassination, including those of General Mohamadvali Gharani, the first chief of staff of the revolutionary regime and Ayatollah Morteza Motahari, reportedly a member of the Revolutionary Council, in April 23 and on May 1 respectively, underscore the complexity of the task of reconstructing the security forces. The continuing opposition of organized guerrilla groups on the one hand and the awareness of the new regime of the inherent risk of a reconstructed military establishment on the other, further compound this task.

As of this writing the revolution tribunals have ordered the execution of some 200 men, including a former prime minister, four cabinet ministers, twenty-eight generals, and several senators and Majlis deputies. Almost from the outset these executions have been a bone of contention between the provisional government and Khomeini's Revolutionary Council. For instance, the tribunals were set up outside the ministry of justice, which has always supervised law enforcement by virtue of its legislative authority to adjudicate the law, appoint prosecutors, judges and define criminal and civil court jurisdiction.

In the first fortnight of the provisional revolutionary government these trials and executions were conducted in virtual secrecy and often without the knowledge of the prime minister and his minister of justice. The prime minister, unhappy and embarrassed over these trials, (which he once described as a "disgrace to the revolution and against religious tenets"), threatened to resign at least twice in March and thereby forced Khomeini to suspend the trials until a code of revolutionary trials could be prepared and publicized. Three weeks later when the trials were resumed with a vengeance there was still no resolution of the issue of the relationship between the Revolutionary Tribunals, and specifically the revolutionary prosecutor — general Mehdi Hadavi, and the provisional government and its ministry of justice.

These trials have been conducted in accordance with Islamic codes of Justice, in which such crimes as corruption on earth or war against God are punishable by death. Indeed, these have been the most common charges against many collaborators of the former regime, including the last three heads of Savak, a former Tehran mayor and two former Speakers of the Majlis. The defendants were not provided legal counsel nor were they permitted to call witnesses. Once a verdict was announced, no appeal was possible, and the sentences were swiftly carried out.

In defense of these summary trials and executions the Revolutionary authorities offered two main arguments. One was that the army's top leadership was responsible for thousands of civilian casualties during the martial law and that it was necessary to eliminate them lest they attempt a coup d'etat of the kind that restored the Shah to his throne in August 1953. The other justification was that the persistent demand for retribution made by survivors of victims of the revolution must be heeded in order to avoid a mass lynching of many more officials, as had occurred in the regicide of 1958 in Baghdad in the course of Iraq's July 14 Revolution. Interestingly enough, the Fedayin, the Mojahedin and the leftist student groups all favored the dispensation of swift revolutionary justice, although they expressed dissatisfaction with other aspects of Khomeini's policies such as his attempt to mollify and reconstruct the armed forces.

It is evident that the question of law and order and the continuation of these trials are related. At the end of April the prime minister appealed for a general amnesty for army and government officials guilty of lesser crimes, in the hope that the many thousands of conscripts and officers who had left their barracks would return to active duty. The more secure the new regime feels, the less pressing will probably be the need for vengeance against officials of the former regime.

The Islamic Republic

The other preoccupation of the revolutionary authorities has been the substance and foundation of a new political system. As noted earlier, by the time that the revolutionary process entered its third stage, all participants of the revolutionary coalition agreed on the overthrow of the monarchy and its replacement by a republican regime. However, there was no consensus about the political content of the proposed republic.

The only two groups which had fairly clear ideas about the kind of Iranian republic they envisioned were the close associates of Khomeini who supported a theocratic Islamic Republic and the leftist students and Fedayin guerrillas who advocated a people's democratic model. In between them were a variety of positions and orientations. The secular National Front and the splinter group, the National Democratic Front, proposed a parliamentary republican system of the Italian or French Vth Republic variety while Marxist groups envisioned a Worker-Peasant people's republic.

Since the new regime strongly felt the need for legitimiza-

95

tion, a referendum was held on March 30-31 to sanction the abolition of the monarchy and the establishment of an Islamic republic. The regime also pledged that its constitution would in due course be put to another plebiscite. The referendum which resulted in a 99.3% affirmative vote was boycotted by both the two main guerrilla organizations and the secular National Democratic Front.

However, other secular groups supported it for two reasons. One was that institutionalization of the revolutionary change required the formal sanction of the populace. The other reason was the pledge for a referendum on the new constitution and the promise of a constituent assembly in which all parties and opinions could exert an influence on the form and content of the Islamic Republic.

What type of political system the term "Islamic republic" entails cannot be fully understood until its constitution is drafted. However, it is possible to review Khomeini's writings and those of his close associates to gain some insight into the concept and its ramifications.

Fundamental to the understanding of this concept is the recognition of three Islamic guiding principles concerning Divine laws and the role of religious leaders (Mojtaheds) as their interpreters.

First, only God, as the Creator, has the right to lay down basic laws on human life. Divine laws are the only basic and binding laws for mankind.

Second, God's laws have been passed through his Messengers in the form of Divine Books (the last being Prophet Mohammad and the holy Qoran) as well as through traditions (Hadith), all of which detail the day-to-day life of Moslems.

Third, only qualified religious leaders (Mojtaheds) are in a position to interpret divine laws and traditions and thus adapt details to current conditions.

Based on these guiding principles, temporal laws will be enacted by a legislature, which according to some of Khomeini's associates, will be a bicameral institution in which an upper house appointed by religious leaders will be dominant.

Allameh Nouri, for example, writing in the Tehran daily Ayandegan on January 16, 1979, said, "that an Islamic government could consist of an Islamic Fatwa council composed of mojtaheds, doctors in Islamic divinity, and Islamic jurists; while an Islamic consultative assembly (parliament) could consist of specialists and men with dignity elected by Moslems and religious minorities. But such a legislative assembly cannot pass laws as a secular law, because of the belief that basic laws for mankind have already been laid down by God. The legislature will only pass 'interpretations' of the basic laws to apply them to modern conditions and requirements in contemporary societies."

Khomeini himself in his treatise, "Velayate Faghih" (Islamic Governance) stresses the unique features of the proposed Islamic government when he writes,

"The Islamic Government does not resemble any other form of government in existence. It is not despotic, hence the head of state cannot play with citizen's life and property. . . Not even the Prophet, nor the Caliphs had such rights. Nor will it be a parliamentary regime in which legislation of laws depends on the will of a handful of people. . . Islamic government is the rule of divine law. . .

Therefore, in an Islamic government instead of a parliament which acts as one of the three branches of government, there will be a planning council which will plan the operation of various ministries in the light of Islamic principles. . ."

Khomeini's treatise does not address itself to the economic foundations of the new state. But here again Allameh Nouri offers some insights, when he writes,

"In Islam there will neither be the collectivism of communism nor the unbridled license of capitalism. While allowing for private ownership, Islam limits property ownership and subjects it to public interest as well as morality. Means of production can be both in public and private ownership, subject to price controls. It seeks a fair distribution of wealth and shuns usury. While avoiding the excesses of capitalism, it also rejects community state-ownership at a level that kills incentives and positive competition. In brief, the Islamic economic system is a moderate one, taking the good points of both communism and capitalism, while rejecting their bad points. Major means of production can be owned by the public, while medium and light industries remain in private ownership."

With regard to the judicial system the proposed republic is expected to follow Islamic jurisprudence under which Islamic law or *Sharia* will be administered through Sharia courts. In practice it means existing civil courts will be abolished and clergymen skilled in Islamic jurisprudence will be appointed for life as judges.

Since Islamic law has specific punishment for most major crimes, the need for a new criminal code will not arise, except that some outdated forms of punishment will be adapted to contemporary standards.

Finally, on the matter of the armed forces, the Islamic Republic seems to advocte an end to compulsory national service. According to the Tehran weekly Omid — e — Iran (January 28, 1979) Khomeini has described the Islamic system in this way: "the best system is the Islamic system which maintains two types of soldiers — voluntary soldiers in peacetime being one. God has urged every citizen to learn military sciences for times of need. . . This could be done by workers and other groups in their spare time. The other is compulsory only in case of Jehad and only if citizens failed to volunteer in large enough numbers, in which case the government will declare compulsory drafting.''

As this brief review indicates, the literal interpretation of the above concepts requires the establishment of a theocratic state based on a single ideology and single political party. Most of the religious groups subscribing to the slogan of "Hizb faghat Hizbollah" (party yes, but soley the party of God) will have no problem accepting a theocratic state. But it is the secular political forces, encompassing numerous groups from left to right of the political spectrum which have already voiced opposition to such a political system.

An analysis of the present political situation indicates that this issue will remain the single most important controversy among the revolutionary coalition. Evidence of erosion of the unity and solidarity of this coalition is growing rapidly. The postponement of both the publication of the Revolutionary Council's draft constitution and the election for a constituent assembly suggests some uncertainty in the Revolutionary Council and in the provisional government. The developing schism on the issue of the Islamic republic may pit secular forces of the National Front and main guerrilla organizations against a loose coalition of religious and bazaari groups, some of whom are organized in the Islamic Republic party.

This emerging polarization will not doubt dominate Iranian politics for the foreseeable future.

Index

101

OPEC, 6
Oveisi, General Gholamali, 57, 62

P

Pahlavi, 19, 64, 74, 77
Pasdarane Ingelab, 91
People's Liberation Army, 91
Persian Gulf, 48
Pooyan, 43

Q

Qajar, 1, 58
Qom, 21, 24, 45, 54
Qoran, 29, 96

R

Ramadan, 52
Rangers, 70
Rastakhiz, 7, 9, 12, 13, 46, 50, 59
Regency Council, 63, 64, 65
Revolutionary Committee, 89, 90
—Constitutional Society, 41
—Council, 42, 44, 64, 75, 90, 91, 92, 98
—Islamic Armed Forces, 91
—Tribunal, 89, 90, 92
Reza Khan, 77

S

Sadighi, Dr. Gholamhossein, 59, 61
Sanandaj, 91
Sanjabi, Dr. Karim, 55, 59, 60, 61
Savak, 93

Sazemane Cherikhaye Fadayee Khalgh, 42
Sharia, 98
Shariati, Dr. Ali, 24
Shariatmadari, Ayatollah Mohammad Kazem, 21, 22, 23, 24, 46, 54
Sharif-Emami, Jaafar, 45, 51, 56, 68
Shia, 19, 20, 21, 22, 23, 24, 25, 46, 58, 61, 73, 75
Singapore, 13, 36
Siyahkal, 42
Socialist Workers Party of Iran, 41
South Africa, 61
South Korea, 36
Spain, 48
Struggle for Freedom, 41

T

Taaziyeh, 29
Tabriz, 46
Taiwan, 36
Taleghani, Ayatollah Mahmoud, 23, 58
Tassua, 60
Tehran University, 56
Tekyeh, 29
Tudeh, 42, 43, 44, 56
Turkey, 12, 23
Turkeman, 91

U, V, W, Y

United Council, 56
Velayate Faghih, 97
White Revolution, 6, 9, 12
Yazdi, Dr. Ibrahim, 90

About the author:

The author has been an observer and student of Iranian politics over the last three decades. In the early 1950's he covered the Iranian political situation as a correspondent of *The Times of London.* After coming to the United Sttes where he received his Ph.D. in political science from the University of California, Berkeley, he continued his research in Iranian politics. His works include a Master's thesis on "The Mossadegh Era," 1958, a book on *The Communist Movement in Iran,* 1966, and the co-authorship of another book on *The Foreign Relations of Iran,* in 1974. Since early 1970 he has spent every summer doing fieldwork in Iran. Research for the present volume was conducted in the field in January, June and July 1978. Samples of his other work have appeared in such scholarly journals as *World Politics, International Journal of Middle East Studies,* and *The Middle East Journal.*

He is presently a professor of government at St. Mary's College of California and a research associate at the Institute of International Studies, University of California, Berkeley.

The fundamental assumption of this study is that the collapse of the Pahlavi monarchy in Iran was the culmination of a yearlong revolutionary upheaval to which many factors had contributed. Political repression, economic mismanagement, alienation of the politically articulate strata of the Iranian population and the failure of various methods to promote participation in a controlled and limited fashion combined to generate a coalition of opposition forces.

This coalition, which originally was non-revolutionary, gradually became radicalized as the regime's half-hearted and belated reform measures convinced the opposition that without the takeover of the state apparatus its aspirations could not be realized. It came to recognize that compromise with the Shah's regime would afford it a breathing spell to regroup its forces and strike back at its adversaries when the imminent threat had abated. Historical experiences of the earlier popularly based rebellions in 1906-1911 and 1950-1953 had convinced even the politically moderate intelligentsia that this time the revolution should complete its full circle by destroying the Pahlavi dynasty.